It wasn't Me, Sir!

For my sons
Byron, Lawrence
and Alex

It wasn't Me, Sir!

THE CHILDHOOD AND SCHOOLDAYS OF BERNARD CARTER

First published in Great Britain in 2012 by The Derby Books Publishing Company Limited, 3 The Parker Centre, Derby, DE21 4SZ.

ISBN 978-1-78091-005-5
Printed and bound by CPI Antony Rowe, Chippenham.

CONTENTS

INTRODUCTION

Writing this book has been both a joy and a memorable journey back to the days of my childhood. Although the majority of events and characters portrayed on the following pages are based on actual happenings and past friends and acquaintances, I have, nevertheless, attempted to protect their true identities by employing fictitious names. I hope therefore, that I will be forgiven for any apparent blunders and trust they will be accepted in the spirit and good humour in which they have been related.

This proviso is included purely to avoid being hauled before a Magistrate and served a sentence of 20 years hard labour in some remote penal colony on the far side of the world, unless it happens to be Port Arthur in Tasmania. I have already been there, and I have to say, it really is quite a nice place.

Bernard F. Carter

1

RELUCTANTLY I ENTER THE 'SYSTEM'

I should imagine that my origin was no different to anyone else insomuch as I awoke one day to find that I had been entered in the great swimming gala for life, and with a fight on my hands. This is, you understand, merely a figure of speech as at the time I did not actually have any hands, only sufficient determination to wriggle my way past Mr Rendell's cocoa-butter barrier to hit the jackpot. On reflection this was quite a feat and possibly my finest hour as far as swimming goes for I have never been much of a swimmer and only just managed to splash and splutter my way across the width of the local swimming baths to get my '1st Learner' certificate, and that is as far as it went. My arrival into this world was I am told, painfully eventful. I of course, was there at the time, but my memory of it is a tad hazy, yet it apparently goaded my father into action as he mounted his trusty steed, a heavy and cumbersome ex-GPO bicycle, to pedal like a man possessed from Wolverhampton where he worked to Derby to view his newly created son and heir. Regardless of the fact that I probably presented myself as a crinkly bawling thing that dribbled from both ends, I think he quite liked me. I not surprisingly had absolutely no idea who he was. I just wanted someone to feed me and switch off that highly irritating light, for I had just spent nine months in dark, sense-deprived isolation and all this commotion was a little too much. People were shouting, 'It's a boy, isn't he wonderful and so cute.' Yes, I was a boy, but I cannot imagine myself as being cute. In all probability it was more than likely that I was slimy, pink, wrinkled and closely resembled a king prawn that had been overlooked in the corner of the salad compartment at the bottom of a fridge. Later in life after years of mixing with the flotsam and jetsam of humanity, I have wondered many times how some people who are so obviously deficient in common sense are able, and presumably unaided, to dress themselves each day! The point I am making is if these people were the pick of the batch in other great gala events, then what on earth must the rest have been like who did not make it, or is it just down to luck? Perhaps it is little more than an Easter Egg Hunt where to be the victor you just have to be in the right place at the right time!

I was reared on Ostermilk because my sister born a couple of years or so before me had greedily claimed all the breast milk, or so the story goes and I was left with nothing. The war had only been over a few weeks and people were still forced to be extremely frugal, but really, powered milk! To this day I have regarded this proper milk denial as a serious set-back in my life and it has provided me with a ready excuse for all sorts of failures and dilemmas that have dogged me over the years. There was, however, some consolation to be had in later life when a letter was unearthed some 50 years on, by which time my mother had died, in which she had written to my father announcing the birth of my sister stating, 'I am afraid it is a girl which I suppose you will like'. The disappointed tone of the letter seemed to suggest that she had expected something less troublesome or even more spectacular like a Jack Russell terrier, or a goldfish perhaps, or dare I say it…a boy!

Time passed and the family with me in tow moved into the show house on a newly built Corporation Housing Estate in Chaddesden on the northern suburbs of Derby. Every week the rent man knocked on the door, took money off my mother, licked his pencil, wrote something in a note book, stuck the pencil back behind his ear and departed with a cheery goodbye. Meanwhile, with little else to do, I had embarked upon filling the endless days by lying on my back in a cot waving my arms and legs about trying desperately to find something of interest to look at on the ceiling, or snoozing away sunny afternoons in a pram outside the front door of home. Apparently this suited me to the extent that on one occasion I was so quiet and contented that I was completely forgotten until the evening when my mother suddenly remembered that I was still outside under the front porch. Perhaps she was secretly hoping someone would take me away and ease the weekly grocery bill and the strain on her ration book. Nobody did. I was here to stay. After a while I was released from both cot and pram for short exercise periods and allowed to crawl around the floor of the living room; and so it was on all fours, my rear end heavily harnessed in swathes of towelling that I developed an intimate knowledge of the lower half of all the chair and table legs in the room. To this day I have not been able to put this knowledge to any practical use. It was during one of these forays on the floor that I discovered the lower shelf of my father's bookcase. With some effort I found I was able to drag several of the books off the shelf in an attempt to quench my thirst for erudition. Alas, being unable to comprehend the written word resulted in an unprecedented urinary outburst that covered most of the books. My father understandably was not best pleased about my quest for knowledge along with the soggy pages of some of his books. I was sentenced to a period of solitary cot confinement. The bookcase did eventually become a part of my life and I well remember so many of their titles ranging from *50 Great War Stories* and *The Ascent of Everest* to *The Book of Baby Dogs* and *Pictures from the Royal Academy, 1894.* The dog book turned out to be collectable, so in later life I sold it as I had always disliked the paintings inside of squat puppies with rolls of fat and wearing pink and blue bows around their blubbery necks. The Academy book I still have and thumb through its pages from time to time. Another book I recall was entitled *The Maid of Orleans* which I once tried to impress my parents by reading as a very young teenager. But in truth it was very heavy going and if I was to be honest I was mainly distracted by the engravings particularly the last one depicting Joan of Arc tied to a stake with flames leaping all around as she raised her arms to heaven looking more than a little put out by her situation. I suspect it was not a day she would look back on with fondness.

As I grew older I was allowed to eat at the table, albeit in the confines of a chair that was very high, very constrictive and from which there was no escape. It rendered me helpless and vulnerable and was no doubt the guiding factor that one day inspired my sister to pour my dinner over my head. She eagerly pushed the blame my way when my mother entered the room to investigate why I was exercising my lungs to full capacity and wearing my dinner on my head, in my ears and down the back of my neck. Normally the pair of us played together quite happily with whatever we could find to amuse ourselves with, as toys at that time were in short supply, but fortunately our imaginations always saved the day and rescued us from boredom. My father would occasionally bring home from work short sections of smooth wood which were the left-over bits from the long handles of fruit pickers and pruners he made from which we would construct all manner of things. They had been painted glossy bright red or blue with the occasional pink primer coloured one thrown in for good measure, if these had not already been ear-marked as kindling for the living room fire. I never much cared for these pink ones as I thought them to be a bit of a sissy colour and would always try to push them onto my sister as we squabbled over the brightly coloured ones. Yet despite the predictable infantile bickering that accompanied play I was rather miffed when she suddenly upped-sticks and went off to school and I was left to my own devices. Now I could have all the wooden blocks I wanted, but playing alone lacked the cut and thrust of a good quarrel, so I held a protest meeting with my mother who appreciating my dilemma, promptly bundled me off to nursery school.

I was young, I was innocent and completely unaware that I had now unwittingly entered the 'SYSTEM' from which there is no escape and no respite as it doggedly pursues you throughout your life. It continually throws form after form at you which you are obliged to fill in, creating masses of paperwork as demands are made upon you to constantly acknowledge who you are, how old you are, where you live, what work you do if any; are you married, single, a criminal, an axe murderer? Have you a licence for this, that or the other? In fact there are forms to cover every eventuality requesting details of all but the most intimate aspects of your life and sometimes even these sacred areas are plundered. Try as you might you can never really shake it off for long as it seeks you out with the searching qualities of anti-freeze. The final and only solution is death and then you simply leave another additional mass of forms to your already overburdened nearest and dearest to deal with. They in turn curse you because your insurance policies are not in the drawer you said they would be and have to ransack the house looking for them. Tiddles your furry feline pet and pal has been overlooked in the resulting mayhem and mistakenly locked in the house for a week where in desperation he has clawed, shredded and partly devoured the side of what was once your favourite armchair and defecated on the rest; and who in God's name is going to have to find the money for this massively overdue unpaid gas bill? If I had known all this when I was born, I think I would have raised one fat stubby digit at the world, turned around and gone back inside. That really is the one place the 'SYSTEM' cannot get at you. It is the safest place to be, except that long term it could become claustrophobic, inconvenient and a source of wonderment to others.

Nursery school was only at the end of my street and formed a small part of a complex of buildings that housed the infant and junior schools where in time I would learn to survive. On my first day my mother left me with a carer and I was suddenly confronted with my first piece of real orderliness. I was told that everything I was to encounter within this building that bore the image of a red chair upon it was my responsibility and could not be used by anyone else. It started upon my arrival with a coat hook, then a beaker, a plate and a blanket. Was I really ready for all this complexity in my life? There was no going back now and although I took it all in it was not long before I became confused as I entered a room with other children to listen to a story. All of the chairs were simply plain wood and not a red one in sight. How would I know which one was mine? You can, I hope, sympathise with my dilemma. It must have been at this precise moment that I realised my expectations of life would not always be met and hoped that crying would solve the problem. In a way it did, for a girl called Pat Cully came to my rescue and attached herself to me while at the same time exhibiting prematurely advanced maternal instincts as she constantly fussed around me, even helping me to put my coat on when it was time to go home. Pat's mother thought this was terribly sweet so I got invited to Pat's house for tea where we sat side by side on a sofa watching children's television and eating fish-paste sandwiches and jam tarts. This was really my first experience of social intercourse beyond the four walls of home and I was pretty keen to keep it going because my parents did not own a television, so for this reason alone it made Pat Cully an attractive proposition. On the other hand, fish-paste sandwiches killed off any thoughts of a blossoming romance, but Pat continued to attend me like an Egyptian slave girl and I felt I should encourage her in her new found career.

My time in the nursery passed slowly as we were taught the rudimentary necessities like hand-washing, hair combing and sitting properly on the lavatory seat and time simply drifted away in a haze of stories, play and sleep. Every afternoon after lunch we would haul out our folding beds and settle down beneath our individual blankets for a short nap. Some girls and boys did fall asleep, some spent the time giggling while others engaged in whispering until being told to be quiet by a teacher who had the 'shushing' power of a punctured lorry tyre. And so it came to pass that one afternoon and for reasons I no longer remember while lying beneath my blanket with the familiar red chair emblazoned upon it, I wet myself. At first it was warm and comforting, but soon deteriorated into a cold clammy sensation which I found disagreeable and raised the alarm. I was dragged off to the washroom by an attendant wearing the expression of someone who had just lost enthusiasm for their career choice who sluiced me down before dressing me in the nursery's 'emergency clothes'. These were neither stylish, nor even a good fit and to be perfectly honest they really were 'so last year', and coupled with a faint lingering whiff of someone else's urine seemed enough to make my friend Pat take stock of her devotion towards me. I suspect young love died that day. The days wore on and Pat displayed her fickleness by turning her attentions to a boy called Gordon Beechey who was once discovered harbouring a black-current, fruit pastille behind one ear. This could be construed as a mark of individuality or else he had just forgotten where his mouth was. This revelation earned him a trip to the washroom, but it failed to quash Pat's amorous attentions. 'C'est la vie' thought I, well perhaps not those exact words for I was only four years old and had not actually considered adding French to my rather limited English vocabulary.

However, time passed in a predictable manner at the nursery school until one day a smiling and attractive young nursery teacher called Jean arrived on the scene and quickly became the centre of attention, because she was adventurously playful and always seemed happy to be invited home for tea. We all loved Miss Jean and one day in a flurry of uncontrolled excitement I along with a group of boys tied Miss Jean to a tree in the playground. For us it was the best game we had yet played and she just laughed and smiled as we whooped and screamed with delight while poking her with our grubby little fingers. I did not consider, or was even aware that tying a young nubile girl to a tree had possibly awakened within me the dark primeval rumblings of a time when men clad only in animal loin cloths would club a woman over the head before dragging her by the hair back to his cave as a trophy. Something in my DNA made it a very enjoyable game and not being familiar with words like 'bondage' and 'lust' I was far too young to even consider it a missed opportunity. However, it stirred within me sufficient courage to boldly ask Miss Jean home for tea which she readily agreed to. Whether or not my mother had any misgivings about me asking an older woman home for tea I cannot recall, but I felt that I was moving onwards and would soon be leaving behind the innocent, playful and cosseted world of the nursery for the traumas of the infant school which awaited me quite literally around the corner. I feared, quite rightly that everything was about to get a little bit serious.

2

MR ROBERTS WAS 'BILLY THE KID'

S
ummer holidays were over and it was time to enter the infant school. Having already done a stint in the nursery school I was, to a degree, partly institutionalised and consequently had some idea of what might be in store for me. Nevertheless, I stood that first morning in the playground with some fear and trepidation as a mass of mainly unfamiliar faces swarmed about me. The entire complex came under the heading of Roe Farm School where presumably in the distant past somebody had either farmed deer or fish eggs, but had since decided there was more money to be made in rearing kids. All the school buildings were hemmed in by a brick wall topped with iron railings with iron gates set in that were normally guarded by a teacher at the beginning and the end of the day. It was to all intents a prison from which there seemed to be no escape despite the pathetic efforts of a few distraught inmates on that first morning. A handful of children completely traumatised by their new found predicament clung desperately to the railings yelling and screaming themselves almost senseless at the dewy-eyed mothers who had now turned their backs on them. On reflection there was an element of 'Death

Row' about the whole scenario and teachers were sent forth to peel them off the railings and make them stand blubbering and whimpering in line with the rest of us as we waited for registration to commence. These would be the kids instantly singled out by the 'harder' element to suffer the jibes and taunts as fingers were pointed at them to the accompaniment of 'Mardy, mardy, mustard, can't eat a custard' which had the desired result of inflaming the situation further and more wailing and crying filled the air.

A teacher would drag out a culprit who tried in vain to protest his innocence with those immortal words, 'It wasn't me, Sir!' Words that would be constantly uttered throughout my school life by legions of pupils, myself included, who thought themselves to be wrongly accused of all manner of petty misdemeanours. The teacher, well versed in child psychology, normally found that a good slap on the head brought most situations to a satisfactory conclusion. Once we had answered to our names being called out we shuffled forward, heads hanging down like Napoleon's troops retreating from Moscow as we entered for the very first time a proper classroom where we would be forced to learn things whether we wanted to or not. Although I was totally unaware of it at the time, this in itself was a lesson for throughout our lives we are confronted with choices on all manner of things, but quite often it is people or circumstances that make the choice for us whether we like it or not. And so ensnared within the four walls of the classroom and with our freedom gone we were obligated to have our brains worked and stretched beyond all imaginable limits as a collection of willing teachers, ever hopeful, attempted to turn us into intelligent human beings. In short, we had no say in the matter. It had all been preordained.

Immediately after registration the day would get underway with us all trooping off to the big hall for morning assembly. In truth the big hall was not really all that big. It just looked big because I was so small. In fact everything in life either looked big or appeared to be far away, a phenomenon I once put to the test. For reasons I cannot recall I was forced to stay for school dinner, a prospect I found myself unable to cope with. The very idea of having to eat a meal at a table with unknown children struck fear in me, so I decided I would simply disappear. How hard could it be, I thought to myself when everything is so big and so far away to hide out for a while? The school was only a hundred yards or so from the end of my street, so as was normal I walked there alone, except instead of going through the big, green gate I hid myself by the north side of the school wall that was less frequented by people, and here I loitered. In fact I loitered throughout the entire morning and lunch hour slowly circumnavigating the periphery of the school wall in the belief that I was too far away to be spotted by anyone given that my head did not even reach the top of the wall.

Ridiculous as my plan now seems, I was not actually discovered by anyone in the school and the few grown-ups that had passed me on the pavement during the morning never bothered to enquire as to why someone of my tender age appeared to be on the wrong side of the wall. In the times we live in now of course, it would probably have been an entirely different story. I would in all likelihood have been kidnapped by a furtive character bearing sweets and forced into years of child slave labour working all hours making cheap shirts in a factory somewhere in the Far East. On the surface this might have had more immediate appeal than attending school dinner, or having to slog it through a morning arithmetic lesson, but I guess in reality I would have missed not being able to play at the weekends and also my favourite dinner at home of jellied veal and chips followed by baked jam-roll with custard. As it turned out no harm befell me during my morning of skulking outside the school and so towards the end of lunch break I slipped back in through a back gate unnoticed to join the thronging mass in the playground. Back in the classroom when afternoon registration was called I answered to my name and the teacher never even enquired as to my whereabouts that morning. I felt like the invisible man (well, boy) as my absence had passed unobserved and unreported. When the bell rang at the end of the day I returned home as usual as if it had just been another uneventful day at school. In my role of the Scarlet Pimpernel I had overlooked the fact that it was Monday and I always had rissoles for tea on a Monday. I really hated rissoles. Rissoles always looked like an accident in the frying pan. I bet they never had rissoles for tea in the shirt factory. I did stay for school dinners a few times afterwards, but that was later on when I was in the junior school. Then I ate with everyone else in the canteen at the bottom of the school field which, rather oddly, doubled in the evenings as the local lending library. Because the entire room always smelt of that 'school dinner boiled cabbage' aroma I often wondered if this objectionable pong invaded the nostrils of the reader when they first opened the pages of a new thriller or romance. I think the smell of old boiled cabbage would certainly take the edge off the latter.

Anyway, getting back to the subject of the big or not so big school hall, it always smelt strongly of floor polish and sweaty, unwashed bodies. The latter aroma was a result of the hall having to double as the exercise room where the unmistakable smell of kids puffing and panting through a regime of odour inducing exercises caused a whiffy aftermath to occupy the hall and assault the nostrils on a daily basis. During these sessions we took advantage of the highly polished floor as it enabled us to noisily squeak and screech unnecessarily with our crepe-soled plimsolls as we jumped, bumped and clumped about like demented Neanderthalls in the knowledge that we were keeping healthy. The noise of course irritated the teacher to the point where he made it perfectly clear that he would employ the use of a plimsoll on our backsides which would, we were assured, produce a different sort of noise from the recipient.

Fear instantly produced silence. There was one particular occasion when I unwittingly became the centre of attention in the hall, but it had nothing to do with PE. It was without a doubt quite physical but not at all educational.

The incident manifested itself one morning when I came down for breakfast. I was feeling a bit unwell and complained to my mother of a pain in my stomach. I blamed it on the sardines that I had eaten for tea the night before as they had been in oil and not the more manageable tomato sauce I was used to. Reluctantly I was packed off to school and after registration made my way to the school hall for assembly and a bit of hymn singing. We had just launched into a notably painful and tuneless rendition of *All things bright and beautiful* when without warning I suddenly arched forward and 'gluuuurrrrpp' out came a stream of vomit which was neither bright nor beautiful. Not surprisingly this put an immediate end to the mass caterwauling as the kids around me rapidly backed off. Girls with hands clasped over their mouths starting screaming, 'Miss, Miss, I feel sick!', while the unfortunate victims in front of me complained loudly and bitterly about the sick on the back of their bare legs. I thought this was slightly unreasonable as it was not as though I had done it intentionally. They just happened to be standing in the fall-out zone. I found myself alone like General Custer at the battle of Little Big Horn, surrounded by screaming mayhem, but unlike Custer, I was standing in a pool of nostril wrenching and partly digested regurgitated sardines. An uncomfortable overnight stay in my stomach had changed them considerably and only the fishy stench bore testament to what they had originally been. It was not a pretty sight. It is on occasions like this when you discover just who your real true and trusted friends are, and at that particular point with sick dripping from my chin I discovered that I did not actually have any. However, I barely had time to muse on this fact before 'gluuuurrrrpp' out sprayed part two. It does not require much imagination to realise that by now things were getting very messy. I was very messy, the floor was very messy and chaos ensued as kids tumbled over each other in a bid to get as far away from me as possible just in case part three should put in an unannounced appearance. I was eventually rescued and hauled away by a somewhat disinclined teacher wearing that same 'change of career' look that I had seen once before and after cleaning me up as best she could I was sent home. I did get the rest of the day off from school which was good, but as a future ploy I felt it was not completely satisfactory and needed to be worked on.

The hall was also the venue for more memorable and sometimes serious occasions like the school Nativity play. This was definitely a 'not-to-be-missed' extravaganza of excruciating acting delivered by timid squeaky voices with all the conviction of an automaton running on failing batteries. There was the usual miscellany of colourful characters like the shepherds wearing bed-sheets tied about their heads with a stripy school scarf watching over a sheep on its hands and knees wearing a knitted woollen hat adorned with cotton wool and making noises that seemed to suggest it was undergoing an enema. There was a cow draped in another bed sheet spattered with patches of brown paint and a pair of papier-mache horns fixed to its head by an elastic chin strap. I, of course, knew that the cow was really a boy called Timothy who wore horn-rimmed spectacles that rather detracted from his bovine appearance, a fact which failed to quell his enthusiasm as he repeatedly puckered his lips to let out a long 'Moooooooo' as if he was shouting for his mum through a taped-up mouth. His sister Maureen sat cross-legged at the front of the stage showing her knickers and appearing to be very involved with something deep inside one of her nostrils. She was also hugging a sizeable 'teddy bear' which was not in the original script, but Maureen refused at the last minute to go on stage without it. This in turn meant that there would have been nobody to ask the three wise men if they wanted a drink of water because they had come such a long way following a star. I also knew this was a big lie because one of the wise men was David Morley and he lived just down the street from me on the other side of the road. In fact I could see into his kitchen from my front window, and so it seems could my mother. Apparently, Timothy's dad Mr Morley, of Pickwickian stature used to have a strip-wash by his kitchen window. Here my mother observed him wiping down his genitalia over the kitchen sink with a flannel which she said was thoroughly disgusting behaviour and someone should say something to him. My father intimated that perhaps she could stop looking through the window. My mother said she could not help it when she was cleaning the window. We always had very clean windows.

Meanwhile back on stage Mary and Joseph were giving it their all. Joseph who wore his own pyjamas seemed to have had his feet glued to the floor having remained on the same spot throughout the performance. Mary on the other hand was slightly more animated as well as being attractively attired in a pair of curtains with arm-holes cut out and gathered at the waist with a skipping rope. Despite holding hands it was a reserved portrayal of recent parenthood and blindingly obvious that they were far too young to be married let alone anything else. The play was interspersed by cacophonous outbursts of carol singing in which the audience were encouraged to participate, thus adding to the general disharmonious bedlam. Strung out along the side of the hall were a few of the teachers responsible for this spectacle wearing sympathetic smiles and offering the occasional simpering comment of support to anyone within earshot. By now the evening entertainment was drawing to a close, but not before Mary and Joseph, by now unstoppable and hell-bent on bringing the performance to a gripping 'edge of the seat' finale had had their finest thespian hour. To a massed shout of 'Hallelujah' they picked up the baby Jesus (really a plastic doll) and with outstretched arms thrust him towards heaven, oblivious of the missing leg that had become detached and lay abandoned in the crib. This unforgettable theatrical blunder turned into a real show stopper and as the curtains were hurriedly drawn across the stage the audience lapsed into uncontrollable hysterics and clapping that would have done justice to any West End farce. The greatly amused, but nevertheless, proud parents filed out of the hall. They could hardly wait for next Christmas to come around.

On a more solemn note, one morning in early February in 1952 we were all told to gather in the hall because King George VI, the last Emperor of India had passed away and there was to be a two minute silence to show our respect. This was a new experience to all of us and as I stood with my head bowed, I was as bewildered as the next child. After all, I had never heard of him and I presumed that he had never heard of me. I cannot ever remember him coming round to my house or the school and had no idea where he lived. Somebody whispered that he lived in a palace in London. At this stage of my young life I did not even know where London was, but guessed it must be somewhere down the road, at least beyond the shops and the Essoldo cinema. It would have been all the same to me if I had been told that he lived in a palace in Timbuktu. Many years would pass before I was to discover that although London was geographically speaking down the road, Timbukto on the other hand was one hell of a way further down the road! Another serious occasion was when we had to line up outside the hall waiting to go in for a polio jab. The thought of having a needle stuck into my arm did not fill me with excitement, but I stood in the queue with my sleeve rolled up resigned to my fate as the victims that had already been jabbed emerged from the hall. Some were crying, some were whinging and some simply clutched their arm in silence, and if later on in the playground you should happen to fall foul of the school bully he would thump you on the jabbed arm and send you into spasms of blinding agony. However, there was one particular boy who could always be relied upon to clown around at any given opportunity. He came out of the hall and threw himself onto the floor of the corridor tightly gripping his arm, shouting and writhing in what seemed like unbearable agony, that is, until the headmaster came out of his office to see what all the commotion was about. Seeing the boy, he grabbed him by the collar and instantly cured his antics with a sharp slap on the head before disappearing back into his office where he spent much of his time. If you did see the headmaster it was normally because you were in trouble.

The very first time that I entered the headmaster's office was because I was in trouble. My friend Barry had been playing in the cloakroom with me and we had been chasing each other round and round the rows of coat racks when suddenly I skidded on my hobnailed boots and sailed with flailing arms and legs towards a cast iron radiator which I hit with considerable force. I buckled and bashed my face on the unforgiving pipework nearly taking my eye out in the process before crashing to the floor where I lay in great pain wondering what part of outer space I was floating in. After what seemed like an age of swimming stars and flashing white streaks I opened my eyes but could only see out of my right eye as the other remained in a world of darkness. What I saw with my one eye was Barry standing close by with his mouth gaping open and looking utterly gormless, useless and unable to speak anything that might have been remotely helpful. A secondary wave of pain kicked in so my only course of action was to have a good cry, which in turn attracted the attention of a passing teacher, which is how we both finished up in the headmaster's office. After getting over the initial shock and finding that my other eye was beginning to work even though the headmaster seemed to be dissolving in water the interrogation got under way. The headmaster's voice boomed through the foggy haze that clouded my brain along with the ghastly swelling that was clouding my vision, demanding to know just who had initiated this very silly game in the cloakroom. Without hesitation I protested my innocence by telling him, 'It wasn't Me, Sir'. Barry still with a gaping mouth suddenly realised his delicate position in all this and quickly replied, 'It wasn't Me, Sir'. The headmaster gave a long sigh having quickly realised that this, albeit a short interrogation was in fact going nowhere, unlike my increasingly swollen face which was displaying an array of colours that even a chameleon might have found hard to mimic. At this point the headmaster became very aware of the swollen black, yellow and red mess and probably thought that I was in the process of growing a second head. The recognition of this fact struck home for he was getting out of his depth and not knowing how to cope with a boy with two heads sent for my mother. Her knowledge of two-headed people was, I suspect, little better than his, but the upshot of all this was that in view of my demise we were not punished and I went home for the day. The possible second head never materialised and the swelling eventually deflated, but I carried the scar for years and to this day there is a tautness of the skin around my left eye.

The days, weeks and months passed as infant school slowly worked away at our minds. We listened to nursery rhymes without knowing what they meant, heard stories about fairies, but never saw any; had nightmares about a giant who lived at the top of some hitherto unknown horticultural wonder, only to wake up in the night in a pool of your own urine and lived in fear of ever having to cross a bridge in case some horrifying troll-like being should leap out and scare the living daylights out of us. We were taught to chant our way through the alphabet by reading the letter picture cards that adorned the walls of the classroom. These were normally pictures of things we could easily recognise like, A for apple, B for bat (cricket not vampire), C for cat, D for dog, E for elephant, not that we had seen an elephant in the flesh, and so on, and so on, until we came to Z for zebra, equally as rare as an elephant in our neighbourhood, which would bring our mono-tonal chanting to an end. Then we would have to go through the whole recital again and again, and if you did not do it properly, or messed about as one boy did then you were courting trouble. I can readily recall the incident as the boy called Paul Ashby who had already been threatened once by the teacher for making silly noises, chanced his arm a second time by repeating the letters in a squeaky voice which we all found very funny. Not so the teacher. Miss, unlike the rest of us, was not at all amused and Paul was summoned to the front of the class. Before he knew what had hit him Miss had whipped down his shorts, then his underpants, bent him over her knee and laid into his bare buttocks with her hand until he burst into tears. Not surprisingly we were all dumbstruck by this scene and sat petrified with fear. After Miss had finally vent her anger and poor Paul Ashby's rear end was pulsating and glowing like two Belisha beacons, she released him and made him pull up his pants and shorts and rejoin the class. Here he suffered the giggling and taunts of some of the girls who persisted in reminding him that they had seen his 'willy'. I cannot help but wonder what, if any, long term effects it might have had on the poor lad. Did he for example in later life become a sadomasochist and run his own dungeon of extreme pleasures, or did it make him into a shy, retiring introvert who harboured an intense hatred of women, staying at home all the time watching daytime television and getting fat on chocolate digestives? In the present climate it is pretty certain that Miss would have lost her job, been put on the 'Sex Offenders Register' and spent a short, expenses paid stay in one of her Majesty's institutions. When the bell rang for morning play break, Paul was a lonely soul in the playground surrounded by many of his fellow classmates pointing at him and shouting, 'We saw yah bum, we saw yah willy, we saw yah bum, we saw yah willy'. Clemency was unknown in the school playground.

Most playtimes saw a gaggle of girls playing skipping games and singing out songs like 'She is handsome, she is pretty, she is the girl from London city,' or just shrieking, screaming and giggling at each other for whatever reasons make girls shriek, scream and giggle at each other. I along with my pals would maybe kick a ball about, chase each other, or have friendly scraps on the grass. That is until one day and I cannot remember how it started, or even who started it, but a strange happening took place. The news of this happening spread among the boys quicker than a heath fire in the wind and the tubular metal goalposts on the football pitch drew us like iron filings to a magnet. It had been discovered that shinning up the smooth goal posts yielded unexpected delights. In order to get a good grip it was necessary to clasp the pole tightly between the thighs while pushing upwards at the same time with both feet. This intense gripping action caused a hitherto unknown agreeable sensation in the lower regions that amounted to a stirring of what until then had always been a limp appendage. In our innocence we were far too naïve to understand just what was happening down there and did not have a clue as to what possible purpose it could serve either then or in the future, and quite frankly we did not care. How totally ignorant we were of the lethal potential locked away within our loins. How totally oblivious we were of the trouble it would cause us and other people in the years to come. No doubt it is for this reason we wear the cloak of childhood to protect us from experiencing and knowing too many things too early in life.

The result was that at playtime there would be a mad rush for the goalposts as masses of boys swarmed up the poles, euphoric in the new found delight and grinning inanely at each other wearing expressions on their faces that seemed not quite of this world. To the casual observer this curious spectacle might have reminded them of a troupe of squabbling baboons as we pushed and shoved each other, jostling for space and sometimes falling off in the melee. The whole fiasco would end abruptly when the bell rang to summon us back to the classroom. As we sloped back across the field there would sometimes be a small and embarrassing bulge in the front of some boys' short trousers that caused the girls to point and giggle while the unfortunate exhibitor somewhat confused and red-faced had to simply wait for the tide to go out. While waiting in a line outside the classroom ready to go inside, matters were often made even worse by a very pretty girl called Pauline Charman. She had flowing brown tresses and large eyes and would I am sure, break many a heart in her adult life. If Pauline took a fancy to you as she once did to me, then she would saunter down the line put her arms around your neck and kiss you. Now the thing is, this was no ordinary kiss for she would stick her tongue inside your mouth and wiggle it about which as I recall, seemed to create a milder form of 'goalpost syndrome'. Where she learnt to kiss like that being so young is enough to make the mind boggle, but she certainly had all the makings of a real floosie! If only we boys knew back then what we know now then sweet Pauline would certainly have had her work cut out as she fired up the waiting line of young boys. I wonder where you are now Pauline Charman?

The school year was coming to an end, but not before we had undergone the horror and humiliation of the school Sports Day and the 'never-to-be-repeated' classic moments that come with a bunch of children who are, for the most part, being made to participate in activities by using their arms and legs which they are quite often incapable of controlling or coordinating. And so it came to be that one sunny afternoon in early summer the entire charade was acted out on the playing field before an enthusiastic audience of doting mothers, fathers who did not want to be there because they were missing the cricket on their black and white televisions, and younger siblings that either cried, fidgeted or ran into the middle of an event causing mayhem. The headmaster who on this social occasion had forsaken the sanctuary of his office and appeared on the field looking very pasty through too much time indoors, well in his office to be exact, took charge to announce the first race of the day.

Race No1. The running race. Strung out along the starting line was a motley collection of children of varying shapes and sizes, but mainly skinny ones with thin arms hanging from baggy vests and thin legs dangling from baggy shorts. Everyone wore the ubiquitous black plimsoll which were generally not very black due to neglect and terminally sweaty. Poised rigid as if they had all been injected with quick setting cement they waited for the off. The exception of course was Christine Farley. Christine Farley wore thick-lensed glasses and being somewhat chubby her legs rubbed together. She had only just arrived and appeared to be out of puff just getting to the starting line and was obviously not in a good mood. Mr Roberts who thought he was Billy the Kid stood by with his cap gun raised at the ready. 'On your marks' he yelled 'Get set' and click, 'Go' he bellowed as the gun failed to go off. But no matter for the stampede had begun and a mass of flailing arms and legs thumped and clumped their way down the field, except for Christine Farley who fell at the starting line saying she had twisted her ankle and could not get up. Meanwhile, Mr Roberts was still wrestling with the starting pistol when it suddenly and unexpectedly went off, which had it been a real gun then Mr Roberts would have been lying dead at the starting line having shot himself in the face. The bang failed to move Christine Farley who now said her leg was broken. By now the puffing, panting, gasping rabble had disintegrated into heaps as many fell over each other, some rolled about complaining of stitch, and Andrew Beazley was in mid tantrum because Dennis Baker had tripped him up and now his leg was really hurting. Predictably when Dennis Baker was asked by a teacher if this was true, he replied, 'It wasn't Me, Sir'. The truth of the matter was that nobody bothered to make much of an effort because Micheal Watson was the fastest kid in the school and he always won the running race.

Race No2. The three-legged race. The very idea that two people should be tied together at the ankles then made to run could only have been conceived by somebody who once did contract work for the Spanish Inquisition. There was the usual squabbling and whinging from the very start. One girl was having a major sulk because she had been tied to Susan Parker and she hated Susan Parker because Susan Parker had spat in her face yesterday in the playground so they were no longer friends. Another girl whined at having been tied to Pamela Green because she said Pamela Green was smelly which is why nobody liked her. Eventually everyone was ready, so once again Mr 'Billy the Kid' Roberts raised the gun and shouted, 'Ready, Steady,…click…Go', and off they all staggered. Mr Roberts was by now getting visibly irritated at his failure to make the gun fire and totally unaware of the bonus entertainment he was providing for the parent spectators. On the field the three-legged race had quickly developed into a shambles with very few pairs still upright. Some lay on the ground saying they had broken a leg and others moaned that they had been tied together too tightly and were in mind-numbing pain and could not possibly go any further. There were the usual accusations of being pushed which would have been hard to prove as they all behaved as if they were drunk on the deck of a particularly rough ferry crossing in the Irish Sea. Stoically, Mary Whitfield with her sister Carol made it across the finishing line and won the race. But then, they always did.

Race No3. The sack race. Another equally fiendish invention. Stick a child inside a sack and make them on pain of death get from A to B as quickly as possible by whatever means. On the face of it your options are pretty limited as there is not a lot you can do inside a sack to propel yourself along, unless you can do handstands and back-flips and be a complete show-off. It seemed that more time was spent falling over and getting up again than there was actually moving forwards. Christine Farley who you will remember had allegedly twisted her ankle then broken her leg was a competitor in this race and filled her sack to capacity. She only managed to jump a couple of yards before stopping and refusing to go any further on the grounds that all that jumping up and down was making her feel sick. As nobody was at all keen to see what Christine had just eaten for lunch she was excused the race. Mr Roberts was nowhere to be seen at the start of this race and another teacher had to stand in for him without a gun. After much crashing and tumbling about the clear winner and surprise of the day was little Janet White who was so diminutive as to be barely able to see above the top of her sack, but this did not hinder her as she rocketed down the field, a supersonic blur of hessian that set a new school record. Her performance was so amazing that had she been in the Olympics she would have been hauled to one side and tested for drugs, or even on suspicion of being part Kangaroo.

Race No4. The wheelbarrow race. The ultimate in undignified humiliation. This was to be a mixed race which started surprisingly well. The only competitor to play up was Gillian Hill who started to cry as she did not want to push Donald Cooper because as he was the wheelbarrow she could see inside his baggy shorts and it was all a bit 'yeuky', and anyway he always smelt of wee. Miss Bower stepped in and tried to placate her by suggesting that she could be the wheelbarrow and Donald could push her. This did not go down well either. Gillian said that Donald's hands would smell of wee and by holding her ankles that in turn would make her socks smell of wee, and as if that was not bad enough she objected to Donald looking at her knickers as he held her legs up in the air. All this was holding up the start of the race and so Miss Bower sent the pair of them off the field and was now feeling sufficiently stressed to contemplate asking Mr Roberts if she could borrow his gun and shoot herself in the head, not that it was likely to have fired. Fortunately for everyone, the elusive Mr Roberts reappeared having apparently excused himself to go and do something 'technical' with the gun. He strode across the field wearing a smug expression and brimming with confidence. If this was going to be the shoot-out at the 'OK Corral' then he was your man. As he raised the gun for the final time all eyes were on him. A hush descended over the sports field and a bundle of tumbleweed rolled past him, blown by a hot desert wind (not really, I made that bit up). The wheelbarrows and pushers, tense and nervous, fixed their eyes on Mr Roberts waiting for the signal. They saw him narrow his eyes and twitch his trigger finger. 'Get ready' he growled in a menacing voice. 'Get steady' and 'BANG' off went the gun. Everyone was so surprised that nobody moved on the starting line. For a few short-lived moments Mr Roberts revelled in his success as a gunslinger until he realised that the race had not yet got underway, whereupon he turned into a mad man waving his arms around in the air and yelling, 'Go, Go, Go' like some manic marine commander about to take a strategic enemy position. The ungainliness of a wheelbarrow race almost defies description, but after the predictable collapse of numerous wheelbarrows with pushers tumbling on top of them and more collisions than Ben Hur's chariot race a pair finally stumbled over the finishing line, and much to every-one's relief it signalled the end of Sports Day. The frantic cheering and clapping slowly died away with people drifting back home in time for tea, along with a couple of fathers mumbling something about the cricket having finished half an hour ago and not knowing what the score was. And where was I during school sports day? Well apart from being in a couple of races early on I detested competitive organised sports and always have done. Stick me on top of a mountain, hang me off a rock face, or dangle me down a pothole and I am quite content, but sports days left me cold and over my school life I devised numerous schemes that got me out of having to take part.

My time in the infant school had been informative and eventful, yet it was only the beginning for I still had an awful long way to go and there would be plenty of head-scratching along the way. It was also an era of memorable changes. I can still remember all those years ago my father bursting into my bedroom one morning in 1953 to announce that Hillary and Tenzing had conquered Everest and had stood side by side on the roof of the world. I found this tremendously exciting as we were very much an outdoor family and even then, young though I was, I fancied myself as a climber. We would go out somewhere most Sundays after I had given up Sunday school when they stopped handing out picture cards. There seemed no point after that. The Peak District was on our doorstep and this is where we headed by steam train or a red Trent bus. We mainly caught the Rambler's train on a Sunday morning. After catching a bus into town we would pass the bus station, the ice factory and then the paint factory along Siddals Road where a palette of colours spilled out and stained the pavement. I remember that the rear of the paint works bordered an old canal and here the colours ran down the wall and into the water creating snaking ribbons of colours among the reeds. It may not have ranked as a turning point in the history of art, but I would not mind betting that in today's world it would probably have been considered as a serious contender for the 'Turner Prize'. The road was always quiet on a Sunday morning as we walked on past the narrow sloping entrance to the locomotive works to arrive eventually at the station forecourt. From here the 10.40am steam train would haul us to such places as Whatstandwell (return fare, two shillings and sixpence) Matlock Bath (three shillings and seven pence) and away through the dales to Miller's Dale where it was necessary to change trains to continue on to Buxton: and from such places we walked, peered into caves and climbed rocks.

Once my father was tackling a rock face in a disused sandstone quarry at Coxbench when he called out to me to fetch the rope for him as he was feeling a little precarious where he was and needed the security of the rope. I rushed off, got the rope and reappeared on the rock above him that was topped with a steeply sloping bank of loose grit and sand on which I promptly fell over. I skidded to the very lip of the drop and only just managed to stop a split second before launching myself into space and dying terribly young. My heart was pounding and I was rigid with fear as I gazed at the tree tops below me. My father still clinging to the rock somewhere below let out a string of expletives as a shower of grit poured onto his head and down the back of his shirt collar. He was completely unaware of my plight and I sat there thinking I might just wet myself with fright before plummeting to my death, although I did appreciate the ignominy of being found dead with wet underpants. My train of thoughts was rudely interrupted by my father shouting, 'Will you just throw the ruddy rope down'. I detected a strong hint of anger in his voice, so not wishing to compound the situation further and assessing my own dilemma which was serious I complied with his request and threw the rope down. As I was in no position to tie it on to anything it remained coiled and was still coiled when it hurtled past him, but not before clouting him on the side of his head almost dislodging him in the process. The outcome was that my father survived the ordeal, I survived my father's wrath, but he cancelled the planned ascent of the Eiger North Wall the following Sunday and K2 the Sunday after which I thought was grossly unfair. It was to be about a decade later in my late teens before I took up climbing again.

I think that many people, I for one included, thought that the conquering of Everest stole the thunder of the coronation of Elizabeth II which took place a few days later on 2 June. The one thing the coronation did have in its favour was that we all had a day off school which was always going to be a winner in the eyes of most kids. There were street parties, competitions and games. An example of street rivalry was acted out in the school playing field as two streets took part in a fancy dress football match. My father took part as a member of the 'Winchester Wizards' team, suitably dressed in a below-the-knee black frock, black boots, black beret, pince-nez and a shiny black handbag. His show piece was to take out an apple from the bra he was wearing and have a couple of bites during the slack times in the match. Oddly enough, our immediate neighbour Mr Baldry, of whom you will learn more much later on, also wore a frock, boots and beret. Now it is very easy to pass judgement on this sort of exhibitionism, but whether it was merely a harmless coincidence or something more meaningful between them will never be known, but on reflection it is quite difficult for me to prevent the word transvestite from springing to mind. Somebody came in a kilt while another was dressed as a great white hunter because his name was Hunter. Another man dressed as a fisherman with a sou'wester which had nothing to do with his surname, while his neighbour Mr Cooper came as a cowboy, whereas he could have come as a barrel although this might have proved a tad restrictive as well as problematical if he had been knocked over in the heat of the game. Fortunately the Queen herself was busy elsewhere that day, for if she had turned up at the school and seen with her own eyes this group of soccer-playing oddballs as representative of her loyal subjects then I feel sure she would have abdicated there and then and gone into hiding for several decades.

At school we all received a free crested teaspoon and a padded blue or red money box. The money box in the shape of a small book had a slot with backward sloping teeth like those of a shark, so if you changed your mind about the thru'penny piece you were pushing in then it was too late for no way was that slot going to let you have it back. It also had a small hole through which you could poke a tightly rolled 10 shilling note should you ever be lucky enough to get one. If you ever managed a pound note then you felt like you had made it big time and the world was your oyster.

Many streets took part in the 'best decorated street' competition and my street was no exception. My mother played a key role and a street committee decided that we would represent the countries of the commonwealth and her artistic talents were called upon to provide drawings of all the flags of the different countries. These were then enlarged and copied onto the walls of the houses in the street. A lot of work went into this project and everyone pulled their weight in a true neighbourly fashion as red, white and blue bunting was strung across the street to compliment the brightly painted flags on the brick walls. I have no idea what kind of paint was used but it weathered for years and years before fading away, not unlike the commonwealth itself. The upshot of all this was that a few weeks later the entire school piled noisily onto several double-decker buses and we were whisked off to a cinema in the town where we sat enthralled watching a film of the coronation followed by another of the *Ascent of Everest*, all in glorious technicolour! And as if all this was not enough, then very shortly summer holidays would begin. Now they really were fun.

3

Bashing Brains out and other Friendly Games!

Summer holidays meant long, languorous days playing outside in endless sunshine for it never rained during those distant summers, and if it did then I cannot remember as that would spoil the memories. Blistering hot afternoons were sometimes spent lying about on the almost unbearably hot pavement slabs seeing who could prise out the longest strip of moss and soil from between the joints and making a terrible mess only to be threatened by an irate mother wielding a broom. Playing 'Hoop-la' with a couple of worn bicycle tyres was another mindless pastime. We would throw them up and over the top of a street lamp until they caught and dropped to the bottom where they seemed to remain forever. I never did discover who actually removed them. If we had enough pocket money then a cap-bomb would be purchased. This was a heavy metal torpedo-shaped missile that came in two pieces and could be screwed together with a 'gun cap' placed inside. All you had to do was throw it into the air and on landing it would go off with a bang. It was far more reliable than Mr Roberts' sports day gun. A variation would be to make a parachute from a handkerchief by tying string at the four corners and attaching it to the bomb. This gave a slower descent but the bomb would still go bang. The downside of this variation was that eventually it would be thrown into the air with great enthusiasm only for the wind to catch hold of it and blow it onto an overhead wire where it remained totally irretrievable taunting the unfortunate owner for weeks, if not months. It would predictably disappear one day like the bicycle tyres, but we never knew how. The loss of a bomb was greatly lamented, whereas the loss of the handkerchief was of no consequence as a shirt or coat sleeve was readily available to take its place. It would not take long to find something else to occupy us for boredom was never in our vocabulary and we had very active imaginations.

Digging massive holes at the top of my back garden was one such diversion. It required strength, stamina, determination, but above all the ability not to question the purpose of digging a massive hole at the top of my back garden, which strangely enough no one ever did. I am sure there is some obvious Freudian explanation like a subconscious desire to be back in the dark protective womb, or a long forgotten instinct to seek shelter in an underground dwelling, or quite simply that we liked getting dirty. It kept us out of mischief and my father happily relinquished that part of the garden giving him an excuse not to have to bother digging it himself. Teams of boys from the surrounding neighbourhood turned up on a daily basis to dig like demented demons trying to return to the underworld. It was necessary for them to use their fathers' spades, thus giving numerous fathers the excuse not to dig their own gardens either, on the pretext that their spades had gone missing. On reflection we provided a valuable service to all of them by releasing them from their gardening responsibilities and giving them the opportunity to do something else instead, like try out the newly built pub just around the corner. For a while the horticultural standard of the street diminished while the social intercourse expanded as an interest in beer took over.

A few weeks into the summer holidays saw the hole gaining rapidly in depth until it was easily 70ft deep. Well, okay, so it was only seven feet deep, but to us it felt like 70. It was at this point that we hit an underground brook in the hard clay. All we could do was peer in from the top and watch our hard-won labour fill with water. Undaunted, we embarked upon hole No.2 and turned the top of my garden into a replica of the Somme as the soil piled up once more. The only respite from digging came around late afternoon when it was teatime and here a straggle of weary, grimy, sweaty boys covered in dried brown clay wended their way home like a terracotta army on the move. Naturally, we wore this brown veneer for several days as washing before going to bed each night was kept to the bare minimum. In fact washing at any time of the day was kept to a bare minimum and a tide-mark above sleeve level was normal along with the muck behind our ears and on the back of the neck. Washing these bits never occurred to us boys, after all, we could not see it so why bother and anyway washing was not popular and to be avoided at all cost. Bathtime for me was a Friday night ritual and a truly traumatic experience as it required washing everything and everywhere including my hair with the ordeal of stinging shampoo in my eyes and my head being pummelled by my mother who seemed to be under the impression that she was kneading a dollop of dough. Protesting was to no avail and I was forced to sit in a bath of ochre coloured water with a very definite line of brown-grey scum clinging to the sides. Thank goodness it was only once a week. Hair washing, unfortunately could take place more often if it appeared to be noticeably grubby and often the task fell to my reluctant father who would sooner have spent his time reading his most recent acquisition from the library. He would thrust my head into the kitchen sink and vigorously shake my head about as if he was riddling soil as I gasped for breath with the edge of the sink digging into my chest; and to make matters worse the water would either be so cold that it numbed my spinning brain, or so hot that I emerged from the living nightmare with the look of a boiled beetroot. I was always a little suspicious of him washing my hair for I knew my father only performed the task under duress and I also knew that among his library of eclectic literature was a book that gave a blow-by-blow account of how the natives of Borneo shrink the heads of their captives. Therefore, it crossed my mind more than once that perhaps his energetic technique might be stage one of the process and given time my head would shrink to the size of an orange. This was a worrying possibility, never mind the inconvenience caused by not being able to see where I was going beneath my school cap.

While on the subject of baths, there was a time when it became a source of entertainment for any of us who happened to be playing in the street of an evening. First I must explain the necessary technicalities involved in order for you to understand the reason for the phenomenon. On the opposite side of the street from my house was a block of four houses. The middle two had their bathrooms next to each other and so their respective outlet pipes joined a common ventilation pipe that stretched from the ground up to the roofline. Now here comes the clever bit. The boys that lived in these two houses had discovered that if they were both having a bath at the same time then by yelling into the bath overflow hole it could be heard in the other house if the boy put his ear to his overflow hole. And so the result would be something along these lines.

'Dave,…Dave?'

'Wot?'

'Can you hear me?'

'Wot?'

'Can you hear me?'

'Yeah. Can you hear me?'

'Wot?'

'I said can you hear me?'

'Yeah'

'Are you playing out tomorrow?'

'Dun'no yet.'

'Why?'

''Cos I might 'ave to go inta town wiv mi Mam.'

'Wot?'…and so on, and so on, until presumably the bath water became cold and they called it a day. The entire, albeit slightly muffled, conversation had been broadcast to half the street through the top of the ventilation pipe and although it was an undeniably ingenious means of communication, it was never going to be an idea they could sell to the Secret Service!

Anyway, back at the great excavations some serious digging had taken place and we had dug deeper than ever. It was at this point that someone suggested we might be getting near the centre of the earth which could put us in danger of flames and gas and even molten lava bubbling up into our hole. This was a very significant consideration which I have to admit had not really crossed my mind, but we pondered on the matter for at least five minutes. It was not as if any of us had actually been to the centre of the earth, but we had seen pictures of it in a comic and it looked pretty hot. Martin Ford said he was not going to dig any further because if it melted his dad's spade then his dad would get very angry and give him a thick ear. We all called him a 'scaredy-cat' and he went off crying and never came back again. Determined as ever, we carried on despite the impending doom that threatened us deep beneath the hole knowing that at any minute we might all be turned into charcoal nuggets. My neighbour, Roy Baldry solved the situation by producing an old World War II gas mask that he had found in his shed. Nothing could stop us now. The first volunteer strapped on the mask and stood there looking like a cloning experiment that had not quite worked out properly, for he looked part boy and part fly. Leaping into the hole he began to dig with renewed vigour, but emerged within minutes, pulling off the mask to reveal a very red face, streaming with sweat and complaining that he could not see for the glasses had steamed over and he also felt dizzy because he could not breath properly. I tried it on next and failed to last in the hole for any length of time. The mask smelt of sweaty rubber, became slimy inside as the heat steamed over the glasses and I fought for breath thinking how unceremonious it would be to expire in a hole in my own back garden. I clawed the mask off and threw it out of the hole. It had proved itself to be a bit of a non-starter, so we decided there and then to take our chances with whatever the bowels of the earth had in store for us. Gas, fumes, flames, molten lava, we were ready for anything. We did still feel a little vulnerable in our short trousers, after all there was no way of knowing what might fly up our trouser legs, sparks, hot cinders, anything.

That evening we held a celebratory dinner in the hole in aid of our efforts so far. The top was covered over with sticks and some big flattened cardboard boxes. I provided a fireplace in the form of an old gas-lit photographic enlarger I had found in my shed which already had a small chimney on it and looked purpose made for the hole. We lit a fire in it of twigs and dry grass and eight of us crammed into the hole to eat a large plate of chips that my aunt from over the road had cooked for us on the proviso that we let her eldest daughter, my cousin Jane into the hole. Normally girls were too sissy to be let into what was strictly a boy's domain, but we made an exception on this occasion as it seemed a fair trade-off for a plate of chips. It may not have been fine dining, but it was fun, that is until the hole filled with smoke and we could hardly see through smarting eyes and breathing turned to choking. It was a hurried snack as we fought our way out of the hole, gasping for air, coughing, wiping our streaming eyes with grubby hands and all reeking of smoke. Once again a transformation had taken place as most of us were now part boy, part Arbroath Smokie. In the rush to escape a part of the flimsy roof had been knocked into the hole, caught fire and burnt down the rest of the roof. We gathered around and gazed into the awful charred, smoking mess that lay in the bottom of the hole. It was a sad sight and we all lost the will to dig after that. In a way it signified the end of an era and we would all just have to find something else to do.

A week or so later it must have rained. It never rained during those distant summers, but I guess on this occasion it did. One evening my father came home from work and wandered up to the top of the garden. He gazed contemplatively into the hole like a man considering suicide. He returned wearing a look of despair and calmly announced to me that the hole was three quarters full of water and shortly it would be swarming with breeding mosquitos and within days the entire neighbourhood would be wiped out with malaria, so would I get busy the next day and fill the thing in. He had obviously thought the whole thing through and the subtle, menacing threat that I detected in his voice strongly implied that it would be imprudent or even detrimental to my health if I did not comply. For years the ground at the top of the garden bore the tell-tale hollow of a lost excavation and its buried artifacts, namely one burnt out gas-lit photographic enlarger and somebody's hastily abandoned spade. And so we took to the streets in search of new entertainments. However, there was a section of the hole that had been secretly tunnelled beneath the concrete garden path which had been boarded over and never filled in and remained undiscovered until some 30 or so years later. I was on a visit home when my mother related the tale of how one day she had been hanging out the washing when suddenly a large crack had appeared in the path where she was standing and over a period of time the concrete path had begun to sink and did I know anything about it? I confessed. I thought it was a wonderful lasting testament to a grubby, soil-stained, hole digging episode of my childhood. My mother, having visions of disappearing forever into eternal darkness clutching a basket of clean washing and a handful of clothes pegs failed to share my sentiment. 'Your father would have to go without clean underpants' she grumbled. I could see her concern.

Playing in the street was a strictly territorial affair. It did not pay to be in the wrong street or even the wrong half of a street unless you had been invited there by whoever held the territory. In short this meant that you played within your adopted parameters unless you harboured a desire to get beaten-up by an unfriendly gang of boys. Minor scuffles did take place now and then, but they rarely developed into anything too serious. It would normally be confined to idiotic threats along the lines of, 'I'm gonna get you after school you fat pig'. I should point out that you did not have to be either fat or remotely porcine in any shape or form. It was simply a general term of abuse unless you were Timothy Smith who was very fat and bore a strong resemblance around the face to a porker. But he was used to the abuse and despite his weight could move remarkably fast in your direction and deal you a hefty punch if he caught up with you, or even worse if he managed to knock you over then he would sit on you. It was no easy task to gasp for mercy with Timothy Smith straddling your chest and compressing your ribs to their limit. So having been called a 'fat pig' or allegedly been seen kissing Gillian Dyles who every boy hated anyway because Gillian Dyles was a 'cry-baby' and spent her time pushing a doll's pram around the street, or accused of some other equally degrading allegation the following retaliation would probably take place.

'Oh yeah, well I'll bash your brains out.'

'Huh, you an' whose army?'

'Don't need an army to bash your brains out.'

'Well I'm gonna' get my gang an' we'll bash your head in, so there!'

'Yeah, yeah, well I'll tell my Dad an' he'll come and bash all your brains out.'

'No he won't 'cos I'll tell my Dad and he's bigger than your Dad and he'll bash him up.'

You will have gathered by now that threatening to bash people's brains out was a national street pastime, but long before it was ever put into practice the stand-off would deteriorate into a stone throwing battle that could be quite dangerous if you happened to be on the receiving end of such a missile. Stones were readily available from front gardens and often the road would be littered with them in the aftermath of a particularly ferocious conflict as if a shower of meteorites had descended from the sky.

I remember incurring an injury by a stone when I once refused to join my neighbour Roy Baldry's 'Black Hand Gang' because I thought it was a bit silly parading the street trying to look menacing by waving a black hand at people. After all, we all had black hands during the day anyway, because as I have already mentioned washing was way down our list of priorities. Unfortunately for me most of the kids in the street had joined this gang and held conspiratorial meetings in Roy Baldry's outside lavatory, so whenever I went to play outside in my garden I was heavily stoned by a jeering mob of Black Hand Gangsters. This displeased my father greatly. Not in sympathy for my predicament but because he was trying to grow in the back garden some tobacco plants which he attended with devoted loyalty. Unfortunately they had become peppered with holes by the onslaught of stones with more than a few leaves reduced to an organic version of Nottingham lace. They were not looking their best. My father thought that by growing his own tobacco leaves it would save him money and so he eventually harvested his stone-ravaged leaves and hung them up to dry in the shed. When he finally stuffed some in his pipe and lit it the smoke and the smell was so ghastly that my mother told him it was like sharing the sitting room with a particularly obnoxious smouldering compost heap. My father not being naturally blessed with an enthusiasm for gardening was somewhat miffed at this response to what, until that moment, he had regarded as his finest horticultural hour. However, he seems to have postponed any ideas he may have harboured for a possible divorce after the man next door Mr Clarkson, an avid pipe smoker himself recommended that my father should try dried hawthorn leaves. I wonder if it was purely coincidental that Mr Clarkson barely reached middle age before laying down his pipe along with everything else forever. My father who did try a pipe of hawthorn leaves, lasted I am pleased to say, considerably longer.

Anyway, it was during one of these mass stoning sessions when somebody scored a direct hit on my temple and an excruciating pain seared across my forehead. With blood streaming down the bridge of my nose and bright lights, coloured rings and spots whizzing before my eyes like a high-speed orrery, I ran back to the house, crashed through the back door into the kitchen clutching my head in pain, fully convinced I was orbiting the earth. I knew then just how Goliath must have felt, not that he had ever come face to face with the stone pelting Black Hand Gang. What we did have in common bearing in mind that I was still very young and diminutive in stature, whereas Goliath was a great brute of a man, was a blinding headache. My headache lasted considerably longer than Goliath's for his was instantly cured by having his head cut off, a remedy I dismissed in favour of an aspirin and a glass of water. My mother, realising that I could have been blinded became somewhat vexed and immediately stopped ironing. She tended to do a lot of ironing. With a face like thunder, she stormed off next door to complain to Roy Baldry's mother. Roy's mother was understandably put out by the incident (she was also ironing at the time) and rushed around to the outside lavatory and broke up the Black Hand Gang there and then banning them all from using the outside lavatory ever again, whatever their needs might be. And that was almost the end of that, but not quite, for some days later my one time friend Richard, who had been a true patriot of the Black Hand Gang, said it was my fault that they had all been told off and that the gang no longer existed, so he was going to bash my brains out. Well, no surprise there then. He pushed me up against the front wall of my house and threatened me with his clenched fist. I, however, was quick enough off the mark in predicting that he was not in a good mood and had not come round to swop stamps with me. Consequently in the interest of self-preservation I had fortuitously armed myself with a house brick. For a moment he hesitated before daring me to hit him with the brick. Unable at that moment in time to come up with any suitable alternative, I brought the brick down on his head and he staggered away. Days later after the lump on his head had gone down we became once more the best of friends; and so with this incident still fresh in our minds I proffer the following as a long overdue solution to world peace. If all the world's leaders and heads of state were to meet somewhere, air their grievances and then hit each other on the head with a house brick then they, like me and Richard would all become friends and live happily ever after. And as for all that 'bashing brains out' business, it was only ever hollow threats for throughout my entire childhood never once did I see anyone with their brains bashed out. True, some children acted as if they had had their brains bashed out or perhaps never had any in the first place, but that was really just their idiosyncratic individualism.

Another tried and tested type of warfare came in the shape of home-made bows and arrows. These we fashioned normally out of the branches of privet which grew in abundance in almost every front garden. Their efficiency was questionable but every now and then a superior one would make its mark and you might be hit in the face by a flying stick. I once found the end of a dart, the pointy bit not the feathery bit, and was able to fix it to my home-made arrow. Now this would have been a very superior and lethal weapon that would easily have taken out King Harold's eye at Hastings. However, due to the fact that I was not present on the battlefield on that fateful day back in 1066 and history records that someone else did the job for me I can only ponder on what might have been. It was also an inferior bow of privet which only powered the heavily tipped arrow a mere few feet that rendered it a wretched failure. My dreams of street domination were shattered as my newly constructed arrow fell to the ground about a yard in front of me. After an hour or so of firing it into the garden gate I decided to abandon my miserably unsuccessful weapon, which in hindsight was the right course of action for had it found its target in somebody's head then I suspect I would have been in extremely serious trouble.

During moments of peace, for life was not always concerned with combat and aggression, most of us did play together quite harmoniously whether it was a simple game of marbles played in the gutter with many disappearing down a drain, skipping with the girls in the road, roller-skating along the pavements in a trail of sparks, or just sharing our toys and of course our 'treasure' boxes. Everyone had a box of treasure that could, in essence contain anything and everything that took your fancy and which you considered to be worth saving. For the most part much of the treasure would fall into the category of useless junk, but we were not that discerning and occasionally something we thought might be of value would be discovered in somebody's coveted box. I am not suggesting anything as grand or as valuable as an early Japanese ivory netsuke, or a funerary figure from a Pharaoh's tomb, or an Aztec pendant of solid gold and turquoise, but something more along the lines of a Robertson's 'Golliwog badge', or some foreign coins, or a *British Birds and their Eggs* cigarette card, or some steel ball-bearings. The latter were always good for smashing other kids' glass marbles during an especially aggressive game. Badges of any sort were always highly prized so any kid worth his salt would wear a jumper that hung down below his knees under the weight of dozens of metal badges. In fact we often wore so much metal it is little wonder we did not constantly face north! I remember one afternoon when Phillip Clarkson, son of the hawthorn leaf smoker came over to my house to show me his treasure box. His family thought themselves to be a little bit 'posh' so Phillip, of course, had a rather 'posh' looking tin as his treasure box. He was younger than me and so did not have the collecting experience behind him that I had, but nevertheless, he did have some quite interesting items in the box. We spent quite a bit of time carefully inspecting everything like connoisseurs before he packed them all away and went home for his tea.

The following morning his mother knocked on our door and told my mother that I had stolen two items from her son's box of goodies. I was hauled into the kitchen and accused of the said crime by two mothers who stood staring at me steely-eyed awaiting my confession. Of course it was now beholden to me to defend my dignity, my honesty and my integrity and I could see no other alternative as I faced the glowering jury than to utter those immortal words, 'It wasn't me', which I repeated several times. I hoped this would run in my favour and spare me a lifetime of pointless rock-breaking on Dartmoor, or transportation to a penal colony in Australia, or even worse, being made to publicly kiss Gillian Dyles and push her doll's pram with her through the streets of my neighbourhood like a marked boy. Luckily for me no further progress was made and the case was closed. The missing items were relegated along with many other great unsolved mysteries that have taunted and puzzled mankind over the years to the dust covered shelves of history. Now the thing is that during my adult life I have lived in many different places and during one of my many moves I managed to lose the cigarette card that depicted the ancient rose-coloured city of Petra in Jordan. The other item was a one cent note issued on 1 July 1941 as legal currency for the Straits Settlements and Malay States. It was only printed on the one side presumably to conserve wartime resources. And how do I know all this? Because I still have that note in my possession. So yes mother, I am afraid it was me after all!

The entire holidays was not always spent at play for now and then my mother would haul me off into town to accompany her on her twice weekly shopping trips if there was no one at home to keep an eye on me. My mother's shopping trips invariably entailed long sessions in the open market by the bus station trawling around endless fabric stalls in search of remnants for her dressmaking. As a customer she was well-known among the stall holders and was not amiss to a bit of bargaining. Personally, I found these fabric forays a tad boring and would wander away only to find myself lost among the plethora of stalls that held a forest of hanging garments, or I would watch the crockery sellers bawling in stentorian tones their wares, throwing plates and saucers into the air with all the skill of a circus performer. I always hoped they would drop and break a few, but they never did. Then suddenly, without warning it would strike. Silently and unseen, merciless, nauseous and clinging like cleavers an unbelievable stench of rotting cadavers would descend upon the market causing people to gasp for air, hold a hand over their mouth and turn green. The sickening pong wreaking havoc upon everyone's nostrils came from a lorry that had left the nearby slaughterhouse loaded with hides or offal and was making its lumbering way past Cockpit Hill and the market leaving in its wake an unseen cloud of utter repugnance. Odious pongs were a part of life in those days. Often when I was playing outside in the street during a hot summer and the wind was blowing from a certain quarter a strong whiff of human excrement would invade the neighbourhood which was blamed on the sewage works at Spondon some distance away. If, however, the stench bore a definite acrid tang then the culprit would be the British Celanese chemical factory. Either way, the stink created the same effect sending mothers rushing to close doors and slam shut windows, while we just picked on some unfortunate under-dog accusing him or her of having filled their pants.

Further material hunting excursions would lead me to the more acceptable world of Midland Drapery. Here my attention was caught by the device that the cashier used which looked like a cylindrical canister that was placed in a tube where a vacuum sucked it up the wall, whereupon it rattled out of earshot and presumably into outer space. A short time afterwards it would clatter back down the tube and magically appear with a receipt and the correct change. The Co-op department store had instead an overhead gadget whereby the customer's money was placed inside a pod which was then screwed onto a device attached to a wire that whisked it away at great speed when a lever was pulled. Like a high-speed cable car it zoomed overhead to a cashier who sorted out the change and sent it back. To a young mind it was fascinating and mesmerising stuff. The latter reminded me of the 'Mekon' in the *Eagle* comic I was sent every week. He was a green alien who whizzed about on an airborne over-sized dinner plate harassing 'Dan Dare' the goody. I wonder if the 'Mekon' got his idea of transport from shopping at the Co-op?

From an early age we always took a family holiday during the summer months. My first holiday ever was only a few years after the war. My father hired a canal boat for a week. It sounds rather grand, but waterway holidays were a new concept and our boat the unpredictable *Magician* was little more than a floating garden shed with a two ring gas stove, a galvanised bucket and an enamel wash bowl. Nestled somewhere in the scant interior lurked the all-important chemical toilet and a spade for the disposal of its contents. My memory of this particular holiday taking into consideration my very young age is little more than a smudge in the very back of my mind. It conjures up a moment of cruising through some parkland and stopping to collect conkers. The park was part of the Sandon estate near Stone and most bizarrely a few decades later I befriended the then Earl of Harrowby and enjoyed many weekends with him in the grandeur of Sandon Hall. How strange life can turn out to be.

The following year we spent in a caravan on the shore of Lake Windermere where I saw my first crayfish in a stream. They were dull, grey and unfriendly looking things that someone told me I could eat if I fancied one. Fortunately I did not fancy one and the corned beef and chips I had for tea that night never tasted better. Another year we spent on a farm near Kendal during that hot summer when myxomatosis was rife among the rabbit population. Everywhere, especially on Potter's Fell where we walked lay dead and dying rabbits with ghastly suppurating bulbous heads. The farmhouse was very old and I would lie in my bed at night listening to the old timbers creaking as they too settled in for the night accompanied by the ticking of a Death Watch beetle. The kitchen looked out over a yard where ducks would gather because the waste water from the kitchen sink ran across the cobbles to a distant drain and they seemed to have a penchant for toothpaste water when we cleaned our teeth. The thing I remember most was the hazardous trip to the outside lavatory which stood some distance away at the end of a narrow path through an area thick with vicious stinging nettles. Among the nettles waiting to rush out and peck at my bare legs was a psychopathic cockerel with which I ran the gauntlet at every trip. I knew if he did not get me then the nettles probably would as I tried to escape him. I often escaped him on the run in and could hide inside the lavatory. The problem was I could see him through a crack in the door strutting confident in the knowledge that he would get me with his menacing beak on the home run. Consequently I was trapped inside a hot wooden shack, buzzing with flies and reeking of Elsanol toilet chemical until the time came when I had to run outside and meet my fate in the form of a maniacal, squawking, flurry of feathers on two legs intent on bringing me down with his cockerel version of a rugby tackle. Possessing a massive bladder and having severe constipation would definitely have been an asset on this particular holiday!

It can sometimes seem strange the things that immediately spring to mind when I recall a particular holiday. I once had a tremendous week in Wales and distinctly remember changing trains at Wrexham and my sister buying a Lyon's Individual Fruit Pie which turned out to contain not only apple but a significant growth of mould. These pies were square and came in their own box costing a mere sixpence. We stayed in a small cottage that had electricity but no running water. The bonus for me was that the garden overlooked a single track railway which was idyllic. Anyway, we all took turns in fetching the water in a bucket from a ferny dell on the opposite side of the main road. In those days this was not a problem, whereas now the road is so busy you would probably be able to stand there long enough to grow a beard, die of thirst, or be marked as something of interest on the next addition of the Ordinance Survey map. Scotland was another popular place and we caught an overnight bus from Derby, changed at Manchester and did not stop until we clambered out of the coach in the middle of the night for a tea stop in a transport café in the wilds of Shap Fell. As there were scores of other coaches stopped it paid to remember the individual livery of your particular coach unless you fancied ending up having a holiday at a destination you had never even considered.

At Glasgow we caught a train to Balloch, then a boat to Balmaha on Loch Lomond where we started to walk along the road to a campsite some miles away. As you can see, you needed stamina in those days just to reach your destination. For mile after mile it poured with rain so my father decided we would seek shelter in a Bed and Breakfast croft he had spotted. Sodden and bedraggled we were greeted by a jolly couple called Malcolm and Jessie and their young daughter Sheena who had an instant crush on me, but we will not go into that just now. Jessie ushered us inside saying, 'Come in, yus come, aye come in yus come'. Unfamiliar as I was to her broad accent I asked my father why it was that she appeared to be very friendly and yet she was calling us all scum. You can work that one out for yourself. The upshot was that we stayed for the rest of the holiday and they gave us a caravan to stay in which was made of green canvas stretched over the frame, the likes of which I have never seen since. It was another great holiday for the sun started to shine and we walked, climbed mountains, cruised the loch, I got the use of a collapsible canoe that not only leaked badly but was also prone to living up to its name by collapsing at the drop of a hat and my sister unwillingly caught a giant Stag beetle down the back of her blouse which sent her into a screaming fit. In true brotherly fashion I went into a laughing fit. Over the years before I broke away on my own we had a miscellany of wonderful family holidays all over Britain using only trains and buses that were always plentiful, reliable and affordable. When I look back on those Arcadian times I realise that so called progress has an awful lot to answer to.

Alas, time the thief of our lives was marching ever onwards and taking me with it. I was about to enter the domain of junior school where everything appeared to be even more seriously serious than I had yet encountered. I was now supposed to adopt a more earnest and committed approach to my education for later on I would be expected to take a proper exam, the much feared '11 plus'. It would separate the learned wheat from the ignorant chaff, namely those who had paid attention during lessons and those who had not paid sufficient attention in class. In my little bemused brain life seemed to me to be complicated enough without being tested against the clock just so somebody could find out whether or not I knew anything worthwhile. As I saw it, I would have been quite happy to have a chat to someone on things I knew about like digging holes, clock-work trains, keeping tadpoles in a jar or even the short life of my pet dog. He escaped from the garden one afternoon, charged up the street all tail and tongue then collided with a passing car, which given the rarity of traffic in those days was no mean feat. Still, I suppose I could be philosophical about it and say that if the tyre's got your name on it…then it was kismet. Actually, it would not really have had his name on it unless I had decided to call the dog Dunlop. But, as I would eventually discover, the exam paper contained a mass of uninteresting questions that required equally uninteresting answers which merely confirmed that my mind had indeed been elsewhere during many of the lessons, a fact that would become a lifelong trait. Daydreaming, fantasizing, not a bit of it. I prefer to call it creative thinking.

4

ON SEEING A GIRL'S 'THINGY'

And so the day arrived and once again I found myself standing in line waiting for my name to be called out armed only with my short experience of life and a new school cap, which like most school caps would spend much of its charmed life airborne at the hands of others. There was no place to hide, and nowhere to run. When my name rang out I was obliged to shout, 'Yes Sir' and again the 'system' swallowed me up for another round, cap and all. Now here is a thing for on the surface the word 'yes' seems such a straightforward, unassuming little word and yet it belies its simplicity. According to a reliable English dictionary it expresses affirmation, agreement or willingness. True, I answered as an affirmation of my presence albeit under duress for not to have done so would have earned me a clout on the head. However, I did not agree to be there and neither was I willing and, to make matters more deceptive, 'yes' can also be an expression of delight or great satisfaction. Well I for one was neither delighted nor greatly satisfied at having to start school and would have preferred to be almost anywhere else. I am fairly certain that if instead we had all been given the option of going home we would have swarmed through the school gates like crazed lemmings and within seconds a deathly hush would have descended over the abandoned playground.

The terms rolled by as I settled into practising my writing, tried to get my head around the arithmetic and concentrate on what was being explained to us on the blackboard. Quite often it all became a little bit too much for me and I would drift away into some 'creative thinking' while attempting to become invisible from the prowling eyes of the teacher; and as if all this was not enough to make me wish I could grow a beard and run off to live on a desert island we were expected to make democratic decisions concerning various responsibilities. These responsibilities amounted to who would take on the roles of ink monitor, window monitor and milk monitor. I must make it clear from the start that all three positions did not come without hitherto unknown hazards, so let us look a little closer at these seemingly simple, innocent tasks.

First off, what could possibly go wrong I hear you say, with a pupil going about the business of filling up the inkwells as he passed from desk to desk? The immediate answer is…plenty, and is based on the following simple equation where, CHILD+INK BOTTLE=DISASTER WAITING TO HAPPEN. For example, a well-timed nudge in the back from a pupil immediately behind the ink monitor would guarantee an unprecedented surge of black ink down the slope of the desk and into the lap of the hapless pupil seated there. He, for it was normally us boys that bore the brunt of such pranks, would spend the rest of the day being taunted for having a black-stained crotch. Pulling the desk away at the precise moment of pouring would normally be enough to decorate the ink monitor with rivulets of dripping ink dribbling down their legs and into their socks. Finally there was the blotting paper scenario. Everyone would be issued with a sheet of blotting paper as we were all taught to write with a scratchy pen that had to be constantly dipped into an inkwell to maintain a flow. Consequently, most of our writing books were splotched and splattered with ink droppings which we duly blotted up with the blotting paper. The idea was to prevent us getting ink smudged on our hands, shirt sleeves and anywhere else that took our fancy. In essence the strategy was sound enough but failed to work as we still managed effortlessly to adorn ourselves with copious amounts of the black stuff. You could take on a sort of tribal look if at the same time you happened to be sporting a collection of fashionable, purple patches of gentian violet denoting that you had ring-worm.

Anyway, when we became bored with a lesson which was frequent, someone would set about rolling bits of blotting paper into balls and push them into their inkwell. Enter the unfortunate ink monitor who spots the ink well brim full of blotting paper balls and reports to the teacher that they are unable to perform their very responsible task of filling this particular ink well. The teacher would then bellow at the pupil and tell him to bring the ink well to the front of the class and clean it out into the waste-paper basket, and not wishing to let an opportune moment pass by would usually give the culprit a smack on the head just for good measure ignoring totally his plea of 'It wasn't me, Sir'. Understandably, this response did not endear the victim to the ink monitor whose days were now numbered. It would be a forgone conclusion that at some time, in some lesson in the not too distant future revenge would be sought. The ill-fated ink monitor would suddenly be hit on the back of the head by an ink-sodden ball of blotting paper, fired with well-practised accuracy and propelled by the springy properties of a wooden ruler. A howl of dismay would alert the teacher, a teacher it has to be said who in all probability was already walking the fine line between madness and insanity who suddenly appeared to be twice the size he was a second ago as he towered over the class demanding that the person responsible make himself known to him instantly. From past experience the culprit would be well aware that he only had two choices, neither of which held much appeal. Choice one was to own up, go to the front of the class where punishment would be meted out by the teacher who willingly showed him another use for a wooden ruler by beating him on the back of his bare legs with it. This was quite painful and stung more than if you had been pushed into a patch of stinging nettles which I suspect has become a long forgotten pastime among schoolboys. Choice two was not to own up which would result in the entire class being kept in during play break. This would not go down at all well and when everyone was finally released the offending culprit would get beaten up in the playground by all the boys in the class.

You never questioned whether or not the whole escapade had been worth it, it was simply a part of school life. If, for example, you were found not to be paying attention during a lesson then a piece of chalk would fly your way and sting you on the face. Where did those teachers hone their skills? Was there I wonder, a chalk throwing range at Teacher Training College where they could master the art by launching endless pieces of chalk at cardboard cut-outs of kids' faces? If you were then daft enough to be caught a second time then it would be the hard wooden block of the blackboard rubber that bounced off your head. Partly dazed, partly in shock and with the usual spinning assortment of galactic bodies floating before your eyes and I speak from personal experience, you would stumble and crash your way among the desks having been ordered to find the missing missile and return it to the teacher. Never for one moment did we ever consider these punishments to be particularly harsh, or unwarranted, or violent, it was just part of being at school and we came to expect it if we stepped out of line. For myself, I was a very shy child and not very confident and tried to avoid trouble as much as possible, but not to the extent of being labelled a 'goody-two-shoes' for even I felt the keen sting of the cane and the ruler on occasions. Even if you tried your hardest to stay away from trouble, it was as searching as a Klondike gold digger and would eventually come looking for you. There really was no escape from being punished. It was simply just a matter of time.

Being a window monitor was not a very demanding role, but one that did require a little skill, a little strength and nerve, for a mistake could be a costly business. The classroom windows were set high in the wall and were only opened when and if the teacher decreed it necessary to ventilate, or not to ventilate. Obviously it was more of a summer job when the classroom became very hot and the kids became very hot and a memorably unpleasant cocktail of chalk dust, sweaty feet, unwashed bodies and classroom cleaner's detergent pervaded the air, thus deeming it very necessary to ventilate in order for the teacher to stave off 'classroom lung'. Opening the window involved wielding a long pole with a hooked end that engaged with a loop on the window frame. This was not the easiest of tasks for a small child. In fact it became a positively hazardous task if that small child happened to be pushed or kicked while waving the ungainly pole about in the air like a deranged angler. Such an incident happened when on one occasion the window monitor was concentrating very hard to locate the loop and was 'dead-legged' by a boy from beneath his desk. The monitor's leg caved in, he fell backwards and the pole threw itself forwards and cracked a pane of glass. This brought forth hoots of delight and derision from the class, but failed to amuse the teacher. He rushed between the rows of desks like a man possessed, grabbed the pole, then the boy by his collar whereupon he slapped him several times across his head for being a 'stupid, clumsy child' heeding not in the slightest the boy's cries of 'It wasn't me, Sir. I was kicked'. The room fell silent after this outburst and oddly enough nobody volunteered to take on the job of window monitor. It was never going to be much of a career anyway.

Lastly we come to the saga of the milk monitor which in essence was probably the best of the three appointments, especially in summer as you would be released early from lessons and the stuffy classroom to sort and collect the crate of milk bottles for the class. Another child, normally a girl as we boys thought it was too sissy, would have to hand out the drinking straws to each of us with sticky hands, the fingers of which had probably spent most of the morning exploring her nose, ears and the inside of her mouth, but we all developed a natural immunity to such things. Once outside we would collect our bottle of milk and drink it, more often than not, to a cacophony of disgusting noises made through the straws accompanied by giggling and laughing. During the winter time, it was a rather different story as the milk monitor would have to leave the warmth of the classroom provided by huge cast-iron radiators to tackle a freezing cold metal crate full of half-frozen milk bottles that were often covered with a layer of snow. Drinking this milk in the depths of winter was a perilous activity which caused unforgettable cranium-splitting bouts of neuralgia that burned through the front of your skull sending you into spasms of moaning and groaning. We staggered about clutching our heads in deliriums of senseless agony as we crashed into each other spilling milk everywhere. After we had recovered from this ordeal we would be herded back into the warm classroom to sit behind our desks blowing noisily into frozen hands making a racket akin to a room full of punctured tyres with some farting noises thrown in for a laugh. A stern teacher with furrowed brow would demand an instant end to the nonsense unless anyone wished to have their hands warmed up by his cane. Nobody took him up on his offer and as an invisible mantle of silence fell upon the room we settled down to the next round of laboured concentration.

The only other remaining vacancy in the school labour exchange that might come your way was to be put in charge of keeping the school nature table in some sort of order. The nature table was, not surprisingly, situated in the corner of the nature room by the door so anybody entering could place their fascinating or dubious specimens on the table. It was here on this one table that a veritable cornucopia of the wonders and magnificence of nature was displayed having been gathered by a miscellany of gungy hands resulting in a truly jaw-dropping, mind-boggling exhibition of the exemplar of nature…and what a sorry sight it was. A typical display might include a battered bird's nest of unknown origin, some sea shells bought from a gift shop in Skegness, a pine cone, the tail feather off a starling and some crumpled leaves from a variety of trees. There could also be a piece of bone looking suspiciously as though it had belonged to someone's Sunday joint, a piece of rock (not the sort with Blackpool running through the middle) along with the tattered remnants of a Cabbage White butterfly that had been beaten to death in mid-air almost to the point of being unrecognisable by a flailing pullover, the only method known to us of collecting butterflies. Spring was always heralded in by a jar crammed with frog spawn taking centre stage on the table which never failed to cause a lot of interest apart from the one time when Thelma Smedley's front tooth stole the show after she had tossed it onto the table one morning in a really bad mood because the tooth fairy had failed to put in an appearance during the night. Now it has to be said, and I would be the first to admit that the general lack-lustre display on the nature table would not have halted Darwin in his tracks, but in all fairness we all lived on a new estate and this was no Galapagos Island and anyway, most of the feral wildlife and natural curiosities indigenous to this area attended the school.

While on the matter of Thelma Smedley's tooth she was lucky insomuch as it had fallen out of its own accord and had not required a trip to the dentist. A trip to the dentist was every schoolchild's nightmare. I had to visit the dentist on more than one occasion which to my mind was a result of not being breast fed when young, thus giving me more than one bad tooth to worry about. The visit meant catching a bus and then being hauled reluctantly across town by my mother to the dreaded building. By an unhappy coincidence the dentist was close to another building that housed children who were not quite like the rest of us which we naturally assumed were the aftermath of the dentist's mistakes. This, as you can imagine, made the situation doubly scary because many of us had witnessed the results in the form of a young girl that lived near my street who we knew attended this 'other building'. She could be spotted most evenings during the summer chug-chugging around the edge of some waste land at the end of my street. With her head hung down and both arms pumping furiously like pistons she would steam along lost in a world of her own. This provided some kids with the opportunity to get in a line behind her and mimic her actions, but thankfully she was oblivious to their mocking and everything else for that matter, whereupon the group would quickly become bored and wander off to find something else to do while she simply carried on chugging round, and round, and round.

Anyway back at the dentist and once inside the waiting room I would fidget uneasily and sit awaiting my turn, listening with fear to the muffled shouting and screaming of the victims coming from within the several torture chambers that led off from the waiting room. Finally my name would be called out and I would enter the brightly lit room where untold fiendish machinations were to unfold at my expense involving a ghastly rubber face mask and a dose of gas. There were only ever two options open to me. I could either climb into the big chair, lie back and be gassed, or I could protest violently by shouting, kicking and flailing my arms around until being firmly held in place by two adults and then be gassed. Resigned to my fate I always chose the quiet option, after all if the drill has your name on it then fate will have its way. With somebody holding a smelly rubber mask over my face and me looking like, but not feeling anywhere near as heroic as, a fighter pilot, I was told to count to 10 whereupon I entered the dark world of gassing. Somewhere around six, for I never got to 10 all the lights went out and it was suddenly night. Shortly after, or that is how it seemed, someone was bellowing in my ear telling me to wake up as it was all over. It was then when I realised that the blurred bright light shining in my face was not my guardian angel and I had not died and gone to a place of peace, calm and goodness for the shrill voice ringing in my ear and penetrating my dazed brain was still insisting that I should wake up. I lay slumped in the chair like a heap of discarded washing until I was eventually helped to my feet and kick-started into action.

Once outside I became aware of what felt like a very large throbbing hole in the front of my face where a tooth had once been and that strange metallic taste of blood in my mouth. Searching carefully with the tip of my tongue I found that there was a very large throbbing hole in the front of my face where a tooth had once been and it was bleeding. It was normal practice after having a tooth extracted to have a woolly scarf wrapped around your lower face highwayman style, not that I was in any fit state to hold up a stagecoach for after all that gassing I could barely hold myself up! The scarf wearing business in those days was regarded as a bit of a status symbol insomuch as it bore testimony to the fact that I had been to the dentist and cheated death. The scarf was the knitted equivalent of the victor's wreath of laurel leaves. Things like this were a kind of rite of passage for boys along with not crying if you had been caned hard, ripped trousers and scabs on your knees to prove that you had fallen out of a tree or collided with a lamp-post on your roller-skates. It was all a part of growing up, experiencing life, competing with your peers and surviving the rigours of childhood.

Lessons became harder as I advanced through the school and consequently I was ill at ease with a few of them, especially arithmetic which just never seemed to add up in my struggling brain. Art and craft on the other hand I did enjoy and always got good marks for my work. I remember one Easter we were all asked in art lesson to draw a picture depicting something to do with Easter for which a prize would be awarded during the end of term assembly. We all set to with great concentration. There was plenty of pencil chewing as tongues lolled out of mouths and bottoms squirmed on seats. Most opted for drawing the ubiquitous Easter egg painted in nightmare colours and patterns, or obese bright yellow chicks with wooden legs and red, razor-sharp beaks that looked more than capable of taking out a small child's eye at the drop of a hat. But I was not going to be so predictable for during one of my 'creative thinking' sessions in class I had decided upon the crucifixion as my subject. I sat at my desk and laboured at my picture of Jesus on the cross. Naturally this subject required some basic knowledge of the human anatomy which at the time had been limited to the occasional glimpses of me in a small mirror at bathtime. Undaunted by vague images in my mind of a skinny undeveloped body, in fact my own skinny undeveloped body, I soldiered on to produce what I thought was a fair attempt at a difficult subject. Admittedly, I ran out of time in the lesson and was unable to give him any feet which may or may not have exacerbated his already unfortunate plight, but I thought overall that this was a minor detail. I was confident of a prize.

The day of the Easter assembly dawned and the entire school gathered in the hall to listen to the Easter service during which we screeched out an appalling tone-deaf rendition of 'There is a green hill far away, without a city wall', as the teachers grimaced at the merciless onslaught on their ears. Then the presentation of the Easter picture competition took place. I was rather depressed to say the least when the first prize went to a gaudy portrayal of a grossly overweight chick and I was nowhere in the running. Not even a mention in dispatches. Afterwards, everybody got their pictures returned to them apart from me. I never saw mine again and was too shy to ask. Now of course I realise that the art teacher had an eye for talent and had spotted the genius behind the drawing and subsequently stole my picture knowing that it would become immensely valuable in future years and lived only for the day when my name would be mentioned in the same breath as the pre-Raphaelites.

Singing every morning in assembly was a ritual that we approached like automatons and did not require any special talent. After all, it was no Hallelujah chorus we were wailing through, but merely a semi-chanting interpretation of the words in the hymn book. One of the lessons in senior school was devoted to music and we were taught, in my case unsuccessfully, about crotchets, quavers, semi-quavers and all manner of strange symbols that related to music on a sheet, provided you were clever enough to understand what they actually meant. For whatever reason I was not clever enough to be able to interpret them, so as far as I was concerned they could have been secret cabalistic symbols and there the matter ended. Then all hell was let loose as we were all forced into learning to play the world's most hated instrument…yes you guessed, the recorder. The recorder is a flute like instrument that you blow into one end while ungodly sounds and a stream of saliva come out of the other. After a few sessions the music teacher under the delusion that some sort of semblance to a tune was being created would maniacally embark upon arranging what he referred to as an 'evening of entertainment' (for this read disharmonious mayhem and purgatory) in the school hall. Parents were expected to attend and be submissively tortured by the sounds of the school recorder band. Few things struck more fear in the hearts of parents than the prospect of attending a recorder concert and there would be an unprecedented outbreak of instant and formerly unknown medical conditions that might hopefully enable them not to have to undergo this living nightmare. To be perfectly honest, even the London Philharmonic Orchestra would have its work cut out to play an interesting version of *Bobby Shafto* so what chance did a bunch of kids have blowing frenziedly on recorders as though they were inflating party balloons? This was never going to be a crowd puller for it was definitely no Last Night of the Proms and after an hour of recorder playing some members of the audience probably hoped it would be their last night on earth! For me the only good that came out of the music lessons was having to learn and sing Blake's *Jerusalem* which I never forgot and would doubtless cast me in a favourable light should I ever wish to undergo a sex change and join the Women's Institute.

Although I was never one to enjoy singing in public I was quite happy to do so on the home front for a lot of singing went on and my mother would be constantly trilling her way through a selection of antiquated music hall songs as she went about her kitchen chores. I remember her one evening happily singing one of her favourite songs that went something along the lines of 'I've got a bonnet trimmed with blue. Do I love him? Yes I do,' being dramatically interrupted by an unnerving 'Whuuuurrmph' as the chip-pan went up in flames. Stopped dead in her tracks she let out a terrifying scream followed by a loud 'Ruddy hell' (my mother never used proper swear words) and began to wave her arms about flapping around the kitchen like a deranged albatross. I was quite young at the time and naturally assumed that the house was on fire, so I heartily joined in with the screaming along with my sister who not wishing to be left out added her own screaming to the ensuing chaos as we all flapped pointlessly around the kitchen. Meanwhile the flaming chip-pan was turning the white distemper on the kitchen ceiling an ominous shade of brown. Obviously no amount of screaming seemed to be having any effect on the situation which was finally brought to a satisfactory conclusion by my mother finding a saucepan lid and slamming it down hard on the chip-pan whereupon all went quiet. Dinner was late that evening.

My father on the other hand expressed himself musically in a more individual manner. Apart from indulging in a lot of whistling (a lot of whistling went off in those days) he altered many of the lyrics to his songs until they became quite daft, non-sensible and bordered on lunacy. My own particular performances began as a small child during socially unacceptable lengthy sessions on the lavatory. I would endlessly let rip with my all-time favourite, 'Cigarettes and whiskey and wild, wild women. They'll drive you crazy, they'll drive you insane' which given my tender age could be put down either to prepubescent unenlightenment or premature wishful thinking. Whatever started me off on this song remains a mystery for at that age I neither smoked, or drank whiskey, or had any experience of wild women apart from Pauline Charman kissing me with her tongue poking about inside my mouth back in infant school. The words of the song of course were a cautionary tale and given the way my adult life developed I should have heeded the warning. But for the time being I was obliviously content to just belt out the song time after time until someone hammered loudly upon the door telling me to hurry up as there was a cross-legged queue forming in the hallway. I have always viewed lavatories at home as a kind of sanctuary where I could sit undisturbed and contemplate whatever needed to be contemplated which often amounted to nothing more than the one ornament sitting on the window sill depicting in porcelain a chubby girl in a striped bathing suit prancing on a beach with words beneath that urged me to 'Enjoy myself like Helen B Merry'. I must have read that message thousands of times before the penny finally dropped! Some people spend their time reading in the lavatory, a practice that I personally find both inappropriate and abhorrent. Why anyone would wish to indulge in literature while slowly marinating in their own fumes is beyond my way of thinking! My father for example, locked himself away to undergo some strange mystical, or for all I know, possibly unspeakable ritual involving a tube of eucalyptus ointment the secret of which, and I can only hope it was of a medical nature, he took to his grave. Perhaps it is better not to dwell on the enigma for which even my mother could offer no explanation.

A welcome diversion from the more serious lessons came in the unlikely guise of cane-work. This allowed me to spend one afternoon a week in the craft room making objects from pliable cane. The idea was to thread pre-soaked cane through pre-drilled holes in plywood bases and produce a plant pot holder or a hanging basket holder, or even a tea tray. You can see already that cane-work had its limitations and we were not going to be making wicker chairs, bed heads or lightweight wardrobes for colonials still flying the flag in some remote tropical outpost of the British Empire. The most advanced item I made was a totally impractical shopping bag with handles so stiff that after only one outing my mother complained it had strained her fingers to the extent that she was uncertain whether she would be able to peel the potatoes for dinner that evening. It was relegated to the utility cupboard and ended its life filled with dusters and tins of shoe polish. On reflection I do not think it unfair to summarise cane-work lessons as an opportunity to produce unfashionable articles that nobody really wanted and could find little use for. However, it had been discovered during a lesson when the teacher was temporarily absent from the room that a short length of cane could be lit by a match and smoked like a cigarette. Of course it smelt absolutely abominable and made you feel pretty queasy into the bargain, in fact bad enough to want to bring up your lunch into someone's newly created plant pot holder. Not that it would have been a useful receptacle even for vomit, but it was a bit of diversionary fun. Unfortunately, classroom diversions can sometimes lead to a situation that is anything but fun.

It was one particular afternoon when we were all supposed to have been hard at work with our reading books when a friend sitting next to me persisted in nudging my arm and with a silly grin on his face told me to look behind. When I turned around I was confronted somewhat unexpectedly by the sight of a girl called Pamela Turnley sitting with her legs apart and her knickers halfway down her legs. As you will appreciate, or possibly not if you have never during your life witnessed such an arresting sight that I found this curiously distracting. After both of us had had a good look we turned back to our reading books. The thing about this was that what she was showing us did not really arouse much interest. We just knew it was a girl's rude bit which is why they wore knickers, beside which I had already seen my cousin's 'thingy' and hers was not very interesting either. She would sometimes parade in the doorway of her outside lavatory to me and my friend Raymond who used to clomp around with a calliper on his leg, not that this has anything to do with this story. Now bottoms we enjoyed seeing, but that bit at the front was a complete mystery to us and to be perfectly honest, I had found more riveting things to occupy me in the local tadpole pond. I always knew where I stood with tadpoles. I knew about tadpoles.

Anyway, this is where it all starts to turn a tad complicated as the incident did not finish in the classroom. Apparently Pamela went home and told her mother that I had told her to take her knickers down, that is Pamela's knickers, not her mother's. The following morning Pamela's mother stormed into the headmaster's office and told him that Pamela had told her that I had told Pamela to take her knickers down. Then my mother was summoned to the headmaster's office to be told by the headmaster that Pamela's mother had been told by Pamela that I had told her to take her knickers down. Are you keeping up with this? I was then hauled out of lessons to explain why I had told Pamela, who had told her mother, who had told the headmaster, who had told my mother, why I had told Pamela to take her knickers down. 'It wasn't me, sir', I answered. 'She's a big liar.' There was a feeling of hopelessness hanging in the air for the headmaster, caught as he was between two irate mothers, who with folded arms were staring an answer out of him. He decided that in the future I should avoid Pamela at all costs and that was that. This was not going to be an easy task considering the fact that not only was Pamela in my class, but she also walked past my house twice a day to and from school. This oversight on his part was pointed out to him. It had not been his finest hour. At this point the headmaster was looking decidedly dejected and seemed to lose interest as though he had been totally overwhelmed by mothers and knickers to the extent that he had lost the will to live. I, on the other hand, was most put out and felt a gross injustice had taken place for it really had not been my fault that Pamela had taken her knickers down. I was innocent and yet the headmaster's decision had been tantamount to branding me, albeit prematurely, a sex pest. By prematurely, I mean of course that I was far too young to be cast in this role and not that I was intending to become a sex pest in later life. I fancy it would have been an unfavourable career choice and anyway I wanted to drive steam engines like my uncle Bert. Some months later after it had all blown over I am pleased to report that the matter had not interrupted my reading abilities, for shortly before the end of the final term I won a prize for reading. It was to be the one and only prize I ever won at school. I was presented with a book entitled *The Little Jeep* which surprise, surprise was about a little jeep that nobody wanted. He wandered about from place to place until a friendly farmer gave him the job of ploughing his fields where he lived happily ever after until presumably he ploughed himself into a state of exhaustion and final oblivion. Maybe he just ran out of petrol.

During the last term a parents' evening was held and my parents went along to see how I had progressed during my time at school. They met the teacher who had awarded me the reading book prize, who in his great wisdom pronounced to my parents that he thought I was a slow starter but not to fear as I would eventually get there. Quite where, or what 'there' was he failed to specify and consequently I was left wondering how, or whether I would recognise 'there' when I reached it. But for now there were more solemn things to dwell upon, mainly having to start senior school which I would have to walk to a mile away and worry about 'the rack', an instrument of torture that older boys had told me about and which awaited us all, along with some very malicious bully-boys. The only consolation was the summer holidays to enjoy before I passed into this other world of hard-bitten, hard-hitting tormentors who were intent on making your life a living hell if they decided they did not like your face.

5

TROLLEYING TO HELL

B y now we were feeling pretty grown-up and spent more time playing in the street and often well after dark. In reality we still had a very long way to go, but as young boys we were growing in confidence, becoming more inventive and more daring in our activities and games. For example a lot of time and ingenuity was spent on building trolleys. These contraptions were built from all manner of scrap materials, wooden planks, pram and pushchair wheels, bits of string, nails and looked as though they could easily shorten your life on the first test run. Trolleys, you understand, did not need an MOT. Trolleys did not require any form of safety features like brakes. Trolleys were sufficiently lethal to require the driver to have a degree of recklessness that bordered on the suicidal, thus making him a prime candidate as a kamikaze pilot had they still been recruiting. Sometimes we would award ourselves the luxury of a cardboard cabin with a slot in the front to see where we were going. This gave it the appearance of a tank and therefore, more menacing to the opposition, for trolley building was extremely competitive. In many ways we were way ahead of the *Mad Max* films and in these fearsome rickety machines we would career downhill at breakneck speeds, unstoppable until it ran out of momentum, or if an emergency stop was needed because the cardboard cabin had flown away or a wheel was working loose then a privet hedge or lamp-post normally provided the answer. The lamp-post was really the last resort as at high speeds it could reduce the trolley to a 'self-assembly kit' and the occupants in dire need of iodine and sticking plasters. It would have to be quite a serious injury to subject ourselves to the horrors of iodine for we always saw the application of iodine, and the stinging pain which accompanied it that sent you into outbursts of howling agony, as more of a threat than a cure.

Privet hedges surrounded almost every front garden in the street and were often terribly abused by fun-loving kids. Apart from their use already mentioned, they worked equally as well for out of control roller skaters and scooter riders. School caps were always tossed over them and quite often the owners followed, landing badly on top of the hedge and breaking it down in the process. This was bad news if you landed in the garden and the owner happened to find you looking for your cap and looking the worse for wear, but not anywhere near as worse for wear as the state of their hedge. They would usually vent their anger and show their disapproval of your attempts to re-shape the hedge by a smack on the head. I once recall an occasion at a birthday party of mine that involved a privet hedge. I was gathered in the front room at home along with my friends when we spotted Donald Whately coming through the front gate. Now Donald Whately had not been invited, so we all charged outside and threw him into the street. Nobody ever really played much with Donald because we thought he was a bit of a loony. Moments later he was back accompanied by his mother who insisted that he be allowed to join the party. I told her that he was not invited and to show our defiance we barricaded the garden gate. Then an extraordinary scene took place whereby Donald's mother intent on his joining my party proceeded to push his head through a small hole in the privet hedge. We massed ranks and pushed him back. But Donald's mother was having none of it and standing her ground continued to thrust his head into the hedge. As you can imagine all this pushing and shoving did little for the appearance of the privet hedge and even less for the state of poor Donald's head which at the time seemed to be of no concern to either party, except Donald who was crying and screaming with privet twigs stuck in his face, in his ears and up his nose. His frenzied mother finally came to her senses suddenly aware of her son's wailing and gave up the lost cause, dragged him out of the hedge and back down the road to his home.

What a truly disgraceful fiasco it had been as well as a birthday party I never forgot. There was a happier side to the party because I had invited a girl from the next street who I liked and often watched her from the back bedroom window going to her outside lavatory. This was not, I hasten to add, either a hobby or a pastime of mine, it was just something I observed when gazing aimlessly out of the bedroom window. Obviously true romance knows no bounds for she bought me a present of a Mr Policeman soap in a box. He looked very jolly in his blue suit, black helmet and black boots. This was a time when I still regarded washing as something to be kept low key if possible, so it was some considerable time before the colours finally washed off and I was left to share my washing and bath times with a now completely naked policeman. I think it is more than likely that in my adult life I may have harboured a passing fantasy about sharing my bath with a naked policewoman (although it never happened) but a naked policeman was something that was best forgotten. Why do horrible things in life like bars of soap always last so long when you are a kid? It was the same when cleaning my teeth. That foul foaming block of Dentifrice in a tin was akin to filling my mouth with soap and also seemed to last forever? Finally the soapy figure lost its form and resembled little more than a slippery white, overfed amoeba and with it went my hopes of a romantic liaison with the girl from the next street and the dream of a first kiss in her outside lavatory. Outside lavatories were rarely used for their original purpose but did become the scene for such things as a kiss or the tentative exploration of our bits and pieces conducted under the guise of playing 'doctors and nurses'. No medical knowledge was required to participate.

Back on the street we all ran amok especially after dark when we often played a game called 'Rosy Apples' which as names go was a bit of a misnomer as it had nothing whatsoever to do with apples, and neither was there anything rosy about it particularly if you were unfortunate enough to get caught. The game simply entailed somebody being 'volunteered', usually a younger boy who would be threatened with having his brains bashed out if he refused. All he had to do was go up to a front door of a house, bang on it loudly and run away as fast as possible. From a nearby hiding place we would secretly watch a perplexed adult open the door to the invisible man. So far, so good. When it happened a second time it became blindingly obvious that the victim of this prank was not in the slightest bit amused and this is where the dare and the danger would unfold as escaping after a third bang on the door became seriously challenging. The adult by now would have got wise to the fact that the perpetrators were merely a bunch of horrible, irritating kids who needed to be taught a lesson, so he would wait behind the door with his hand ready on the latch. We were also wise to that same fact, but the young protesting culprit would be shoved into the garden anyway to carry out the deed a third time under a hail of life-threatening abuse.

It almost goes without saying that barely had his hand touched the door before it flew open to reveal a very angry man whose hand at lightning speed had already shot out from behind the door and grabbed the boy by the scruff of his collar. His other hand he would put to good use by smacking the boy about his head a few times before throwing him out of the garden. The young lad would stagger into the road holding his head and wailing loudly as we all fell into fits of laughter before he stormed off home shouting something about 'bullies' and 'unfair'. Meanwhile the irate man stood at his gate shouting all manner of menacing threats at us shaking his fist and ranting and raving with all the fervour of Hitler giving one of his famous rallying speeches. This just made us laugh even more as we ran away into the shadows of the night.

Another popular game was 'hide and seek' which gave us plenty of scope to utilise the many front gardens and hedges in the street. The rules were simple. The seeker would stand by a lamp-post with closed eyes and count to 100 after which they would shout, 'Coming ready or not'. The hiders would of course have disappeared from sight, but would try to get back to the lamp-post before the seeker could find them or spot them. This meant you were safe from being caught. Because of the ridiculous lengths that some of us would go to in order to conceal ourselves it often meant that the game went on for ages. In fact some kids were never found at all and eventually everyone would give up and play another game or just go home. For all I know some may have remained undiscovered to this day and are still hiding out in an overgrown back garden, lean and skinny with massive beards, raiding waste bins and bird tables under the cover of darkness, nervously watching and waiting like those Japanese soldiers from World War Two who refuse to believe that the war is over and are still in hiding decades on in the jungles of a remote Pacific island. On the other hand, when Fredericks, the local ice cream van turned up sounding its croaky horn then perhaps they would be prepared to blow their cover to join the rest of us harassing the vendor for some free broken cornets.

If it was very sunny and too hot even to play marbles in the gutter and trying to avoid the hazard of a runaway marble disappearing down the road drain forever, then we might just idle away our time making artistic endeavours with a soft stone on the paving slabs, or simply annoy the girls who would be jumping up and down to a skipping rope slung across the road. However, if the great outdoors called then I would grab a couple of pals and head for the fields at the top of the hill. Here we would poke about in the tadpole pond and attempt to push each other in. Famous as it was for frog spawn in spring, I think 'old pram wheels, bicycle frames and bedstead' pond might have been a more accurate name for these inhabited the pond all year round.

I remember an incident one winter passing the frozen pond when my father, an avid photographer and fancying himself on a par with Herbert Ponting suggested that I have my picture taken standing on the ice. Despite lacking the confidence of either Shackleton or Scott I stepped out onto the ice, struck a pose, heard the ice crack and promptly fell in. You will readily understand when I say that the temperature of the water was not conducive to an early morning swim and wading out of the pond with both wellingtons full of iced water was not the sort of pastime that I would recommend unless you are a masochist, have a death wish, or are devoid of anything that might possibly resemble a brain. My father helped me out and I emptied my boots. I felt more than a little disgruntled by the escapade and to make matters worse my father had not even taken the photograph! The words of comfort he proffered as we made our way back home was that it could have been a lot worse if my leg had been bitten off by a shark as I stood in the pond. On reflection it was a pretty bizarre concept but I was too young at the time to tell him that I thought his sanity was questionable. It is more likely that I could have been speared by a piece of rusting, slime covered bicycle or bed-end and died a long, ghastly, lingering death by ptomaine poisoning. It was another winter when my father bought a pair of ex-army skis for a pound off a mate at work and took to the slopes near the pond. We all had a go at making some sort of dignified attempt at going downhill, but it did not take long for it to dawn on us that this was never going to be a number one pastime. When it was my turn I toppled over several times, got in a terrible tangle eventually finishing with the splits. Up until this point in my life I was unaware that I could do the splits. It was a painful experience and in the interests of protecting my undercarriage, I never did the splits ever again!

A couple of fields further on, lay a bluebell wood and a farm orchard surrounded by a high brick wall which with some difficulty we were just able to scale and pilfer a few apples as survival rations. Across from here was a building that was always known as the Bishop's Palace set in wooded grounds and believed by all children to be haunted. What this story was based on is a bit of a mystery for I never knew or heard of anyone who had actually seen a ghost there. To my knowledge nobody had seen the spectre of a semi-transparent bishop whizzing around the grounds with his cloak flying out behind him as he sat astride a crosier, or had witnessed the ghostly gaunt white face of a bishop at a window at twilight, open-mouthed with a bemused expression on his face wondering who that ghost was whizzing around his front lawn astride a crosier. Either way it worked as an extremely good deterrent that kept us at a safe distance from the perimeter fence. From here we crossed a road to a lane descending steeply downhill past The Windmill, a quaint old pub that was everything an old English country pub should be, that is before it became engulfed by what is believed to be the largest housing estate in Europe. The lane ran alongside a high wall behind which sat a large house that my father had told me was a school for naughty girls, a fact that intrigued me for years. He was given to a wild imagination, so despite it taking me a little time when very young to see through his explanation that the far distant cooling towers of a power station had nothing whatsoever to do with treacle mines, on this occasion I believed he was telling me the truth. Anyway, for years I mused on what a school for naughty girls might entail. For example, how naughty did you have to be to qualify as a naughty girl and what kind of naughtiness did naughty girls get up to that landed them here at the naughty girls' school? The questions remained unanswered and whenever I passed the rear of the school, which was often because the lane carried on down to the railway line where I played and waited for trains, I never once caught sight of a naughty girl and I so longed to see one. I wonder whether it was as wild and as wonderful as St Trinians? I would really like to think so.

Breadsall village at the end of the lane was a sanctuary of old cottages with gardens filled with roses, hollyhocks and lupins, a ramshackle forge with a huge heap of rusting horseshoes by its door and a country railway station. This was about the limit of my exploration for it all seemed a hundred miles away from the red rooftops of the estate and home. Getting back home meant following the railway line through a wooded cutting where wild damsons grew which we foolishly picked and ate. They were so unbelievably tart that it felt like your entire face was being sucked into your mouth and devoured. I learnt my mistake first time around as well as realising the improbability of getting home without a face. In such a condition it would have been all too easy to walk into an oncoming train not to mention my mother getting quite vexed if I was late home for tea. Emerging from the cutting I would race my pals to the bottom of the hill by rolling down the railway embankment at great speed through what was basically a slalom course of cow-pats. Then we would cross a road to look for peewit's nests in a swampland of reed grass and black, evil-smelling water. Today this entire area is unrecognisable as it lies beneath a sprawling industrial estate and the railway viaduct that we passed beneath as we stole our way through a private scrap yard was blown up one Sunday morning to make way for a new road scheme.

About half a mile from my house I had to cross a track through an area called the 'tip' made up mainly of slag and cinder presumably from the nearby iron foundry. It was called the tip for good reason as here you could find almost everything that could be tipped including old bicycle frames, old bedsteads, dead cats, bags of old clothes, broken pipes, building rubble, bits of old cars and some more dead cats, in fact anything that was broken, worn out and which people no longer wanted or had use for was here on the tip. I remember one year when a report in the local paper told how a heap of watches had been found on the tip with luminous faces made from a radioactive material that was considered to be harmful. Immediately a crowd of us set off for the tip hoping we could find some that might turn us into powerful, lumbering mutants with perhaps red-spotted, green scaly skin and blobby antenna waving about on the tops of our heads. We could then take over the entire estate by terrifying all the other kids. We knew all about radioactive stuff because we had seen what it could do to you in comics, so it must be true. It was a lot to fit in for one afternoon as we all had to be home in time for tea which I did not want to miss as it was Tuesday and we always had sausages on Tuesday, even though they would be a tad burnt. My father said he quite liked them black which was his good fortune, for when it came to sausages my mother only ever did black! The outcome from all this was that despite searching the tip for ages we only found the usual assortment of rubbish and of course the ubiquitous dead cat.

We returned as we had left, just a little grubbier and probably a bit smellier, not that we noticed. As we mounted the top of the hill that led from the tip, hot, grimy and sweaty it was the final insult to turn the corner of the street and see the Corona 'fizzy pop' lorry unloading a crate of lemonade and orangeade to a house down the street. We gazed at it with our tongues lolling out the sides of our mouths as if we had just crossed the hottest of deserts and had suddenly homed in on an oasis of fizzy life-saving pop. The family who lived in that house were Mormons who we presumed did not drink tea and therefore had to suffer drinking fizzy pop all the time which I for one only drank on extremely rare occasions as a treat. At this stage we did not need anything radioactive to turn us green for envy had already done that as we gaped forlornly at the lorry full of bottles. The only soft drink that I ever had at home was diluted lemon and barley water which looked like dish water and tasted not too dissimilar, not that I was in the habit of drinking dish water. It was pure speculation on my part. I was once allowed a tin of crystals that looked suspiciously like ferricyanide, except when mixed with water it was supposed to make an orange drink and not turn you blue and kill you. There was of course the ubiquitous ginger beer plant that invaded every household with greater rapidity than the Black Death and once installed was difficult to get rid of. In my house it lived on the kitchen window sill as a jar of malevolent rust coloured sediment that now and again burped bubbles. After weeks of continually feeding the ravenous appetite of the sludgy beast and weeks of drinking vast quantities of ginger beer that it produced in a vain effort to keep up with the pace of production, it ended its days by being flushed down the lavatory. I wonder if now, all these decades on whether somewhere in a dark, long forgotten sewer that brown formless dollop of sludge has manifested itself into a hitherto unknown life form that threatens from deep within the sewerage system of every major city throughout the country. Rather deflated we trudged back to our respective homes all too aware that our dream of controlling the estate followed by possible world domination had just flown out of the window. Was life always going to be this cruel?

During the winter we often had heavy falls of that white stuff purpose made for children to enjoy themselves with. The centre of my street would quickly be turned into a shining streak of solid ice with a finish like glass, polished by countless slithering feet as we all made running attacks at the slide. We thought it was great fun and enjoyed every minute on it, whereas the grown-ups viewed it as a death trap especially if you were unfortunate enough not to spot it in time while riding a bicycle along the street. This could have serious consequences and any unfortunate person falling foul of our slide on a bicycle would be better off dispensing with that segment of their life and proceed straight to the undertaker. It was normally only a matter of time before somebody's mother would decide that it was an unnecessary hazard and throw a pan of hot ashes over it and completely ruin the slide. Annoyed, but not daunted we would simply start up somewhere else in the street.

The road that ran along the end of the street rose quite steeply and was used by so many children from all the surrounding streets that it very soon took on the appearance of a shimmering glacier. This was the local toboggan run where seemingly unhinged kids astride a miscellany of home-made contraptions that might loosely be grouped under the heading of sledges, zoomed downhill at suicidal speeds using only their feet as brakes, or as a last resort a lamp-post. What few cars there were at the time tended to find an alternative route to avoid the ice slope, so there was little fear of colliding with anything bigger than you coming the other way at considerable speed! Should you by some unfortunate error of judgement happen to go all the way to the main road at the bottom of the hill, then if you were really quick you might just have time to make out the number plate on the local bus before everything turned black and very quiet. One year a group of particularly foolhardy lads got together and decided to construct a six wheeled trolley and launch it down the ice run. Now in all probability you could write this next bit yourself because the outcome is so predictable, and yet the belief in the indestructability of young life led to the following. The trolley was held back with some difficulty as the driver, he held the steering string, and four other lads got on board. However, before they had managed to settle in properly the trolley shot away at an alarming speed down the ice run. Disaster was imminent and as it gathered even more speed the trolley, due no doubt to sloppy cheap labour jack-knifed partway down the hill catapulting into the air wheels, planks of wood and all manner of airborne bits and pieces along with a jumbled assortment of flailing arms and legs flying in all directions. Pandemonium set in as bodies crashed to the ground accompanied by yelling, screaming, bumped heads and blood. Admittedly there was not a lot of blood, but sufficient to keep the onlookers in good spirits as though they were attending the games in the Coliseum. (The one in Rome that is, not the picture house in town.) The trolley or what was left of it continued on at a great rate of knots before finally veering off to one side to shatter against a lamp-post. The dare-devil boys picked themselves up with a couple sloping off home with torn trousers and bloodied knees to face even further trauma in the shape of an iodine bottle. A group of us gathered around the lamp-post like mourners at a graveside surveying the crumpled wheels and splintered wood that only moments ago had been the very cutting edge of trolley building technology but which had now been reduced to a pile of scrap. It was the Concorde of the trolley world. It had been the first of its kind, revolutionary, inventive and incredibly stupid. Everyone stuck to four wheels after this fiasco and kept well away from ice.

With each fresh fall of snow came the traditional and almost compulsory snowball fights, along with the building of misshapen snowmen that appeared dotted along the pavement like arctic chessmen. My neighbour, Roy Baldry once attempted to construct an igloo in his back garden, which if you have never built one before is quite an ambitious project and in his case doomed to failure. All went well until he tried to slope in the walls which refused to stay in place and simply collapsed. He persevered throughout the day and late in the afternoon he had finally created a snow version of a circular pyramid, which might vaguely have been mistaken for an igloo if you happened to be viewing it from a considerable distance in the teeth of a force 10 blizzard through frozen contact lenses. As a pyramid, well no self-respecting Pharaoh would want to be seen dead in the thing apart from the fact that once it had melted, the Pharaoh might be more than a little disappointed when he realised he had not journeyed to the hereafter as intended, but was in truth still in Roy Baldry's back garden! This was not the promised land.

When everything else had been tried there was always the communal activity of seeing who could roll the biggest snowball in the street. It would need three or four of us to manoeuvre these massive, weighty snowballs once they became a few feet in height. The major problem then was that we could not generally see where we were going, or anything that might be in our path for with heads down and pushing as if our very lives depended on it we were lost to physical exertion and concentration. It would seem that nothing could break the intensity of this challenge except, that is, the moment when a foul smell invaded our nostrils and a tell-tale yellow-brown smudge appeared on the side of the snowball that told us we had collected some over-ripe dog pooh. It would be mere seconds later when one of us would discover that they had stuck their hand in it while rolling the ball. This was the signal to collectively back-off and begin jeering at the unfortunate victim wearing the snow-sodden mittens smeared with dog pooh. The ritual would take the form of us all shouting, 'Dog pooh, dog pooh, you stink of dog pooh'. We were never short of inspired jibes for there was a bit of 'singer-song writer' in all of us. The taunted boy would probably yell back, 'Shurr'up you fat pig' or something equally as damning and rush off home in tears. In those days dog pooh was a constant hazard in the street for dogs were allowed to roam where they liked, bark, fight and copulate whenever they felt the need, so dog pooh was a common sight especially around the bottoms of darkly stained, urine impregnated lamp-posts where generations of dogs had cocked their legs. Dog pooh was also a common sight on the soles of your shoes and if it appeared on the kitchen floor then you would find yourself back outside quicker than you thought possible.

There was one occasion after we had rolled a giant snowball when we decided to play a trick on a scruffy and often smelly kid called Robin Shetley who nobody played with much because he was…well, a bit scruffy and smelly. One evening after dark we rolled the giant snowball and jammed it in the gateway of Robin Shetley's garden. The gate itself had gone missing some time ago and was probably used for firewood, so we thought our snowball should take its place which it did with very hard pushing. The next morning as I scraped away the frost ferns on the inside of my bedroom window I peered out in time to see an incident take place involving the massive snowball. I saw Mr Shetley coming down the road on his bicycle after his night shift on the railway. He came to a halt by the snowball wearing an expression that did not suggest happiness. He dismounted, threw his bicycle to the ground and grabbed the snowball trying to dislodge it with a series of sudden jerking movements. However, he struggled in vain for an overnight frost had frozen it firmly to the ground and the gateposts. He then resorted to manic kicking with his boots but to little effect. By now I could plainly see that he was in a rage because he just wanted a cup of tea, his breakfast and a well-earned sleep. In desperation he got hold of the bicycle pump and began jabbing away at the side of the snowball in a fearful frenzy but in reality was having less success than prehistoric man had picking flints out of the ground with a piece of deer antler. It was after all a bicycle pump and bicycle pumps were designed to make things bigger rather than smaller, but Mr Shetley was fast becoming a desperate man. With a face as red as an erupting volcano complete with steam all but coming out of his ears, he abandoned his trusty steed, an act which at any other time of the year would have delighted the rag and bone man who plodded his horse-drawn wagon around the streets collecting everything and anything that was left on the pavement or propped against a gateway. Finally, Mr Shetley successfully clawed his way through a hole in the hedge. Later that morning Robin Shetley was seen in a very bad mood after having been made to dig out the offending snowball with his father's spade, a task he felt was grossly unfair and which seemed to anger him greatly. We, of course never owned up to the prank especially as Robin was the one furiously wielding a spade.

During the warmer times of the year we would sometimes sneak into the secret grounds of the clinic at the bottom of the school field. Being a part of the school complex it was also surrounded by a brick wall topped with iron railings which we quickly scaled in order not to be spotted by the school caretaker who lived a few yards away and spent much of his evenings pottering around his garden. The clinic grounds were strictly out of bounds to everyone especially during the evening when it was closed behind locked gates. The building was always a mystery to us which made our forays even more daring, because all any of us ever saw going into the place during the day was mothers with pushchairs, but for what purpose we had absolutely no idea. Not knowing what the word clinic actually meant did not help matters, so we assumed that it was some kind of place where experiments were carried out on kids who could only be pushed about in pushchairs either before or after whatever took place inside. You see, mysteries of any sort always fired our imaginations and nothing ever seemed straightforward. Things always had to be linked to some kind of macabre goings on if we did not understand the purpose. The idea never occurred to us that something might be quite simple and sensible.

Anyway, once over the railings we crept about in a twilight world of dense shrubs and bushes and here among the grass we would hunt for pignuts which we clawed out of the earth with our bare hands. It was not as if we were teetering on the brink of starvation for we had only had our tea an hour ago, it was just the same as scrumping apples. We did it because they were there. Pignuts are an edible tuber and are not by any stretch of the imagination to be classed as a gastronomic delight. They are slightly sweet, crunchy and in our case gritty with soil as we could only wipe them over with our very grubby hands. How we ever recognised the pignut umbellifer from a host of similar looking plants is a puzzle, but we rarely got stomach pains and nobody died. I think it was all down to an awakening of our survival genes that relate back to when we were all 'hunter-gatherers' in the days of early man that automatically kicks in when the need arises. Like knowing that on a Wednesday afternoon and all day Sunday when the Co-op was closed you would not be able to get a pignut, or anything else for that matter. Now I come to think of it I do not suppose the Co-op ever did sell pignuts. They did sell grape nuts which was a breakfast cereal not unlike eating a bowl of gravel with milk. They were so hard it made my jaw ache crunching them, chipped my teeth and consisted of neither grapes nor nuts. I guess it really was just gravel. Weetabix were much more preferable and you got a cut-out cardboard lorry on the back to stick together using Seccotine glue. This had a particularly distinctive smell as it was a fish-based liquid glue used for sticking together paper and cardboard and was not a substitute for Shippams fish paste. Nobody would want to spread Seccotine on a slice of bread.

Opposite the clinic was a long, featureless building occupying an area of waste land which was known simply as 'the green' where I sometimes played with my friends. This brick building was another conundrum surrounded by a high chain-link fence with windows of frosted wire-meshed glass that hid its secret from prying eyes. We knew that it had something to do with electricity but did not know what and could do little else but wonder what produced the constant humming noise that emanated from within. Over many years we tried to find out by throwing stones, bricks and lumps of concrete through the windows in an attempt to shine some light on the machines that must be inside. We were good at throwing things. I once spent a pleasant half hour with a lad called Terry throwing eggs from his mother's larder high into the air so they landed with a satisfying splat on the roof of his shed. I have no doubt that his mother came home from work that evening and questioned him about the mysterious disappearance of a dozen eggs. He of course would be unable to throw any light on the matter and no doubt uttered his innocence with 'It wasn't me'. Imagine his mother's surprise when she went to close his bedroom curtains that evening and saw the shed roof decorated with a dozen badly made omelettes. It had been a very hot day and they had cooked on the black bitumen roof. Terry's mother must have found it a striking sight, if not a little unexpected.

Predictably, we imagined the fenced building must have something to do with spaceships and aliens and fiendish experiments especially at night when a light sometimes glowed through the perforated windows. Alas, the windows were too high up the wall so we never did get to see inside, but it served to fuel our vivid imaginations. It was demolished decades ago to make way for houses and I never heard any reports about finding spaceships or aliens. Still, they said the same about Roswell in New Mexico! This green was in reality a wilderness of tall grass, giant weeds and sprawling colonies of nettles, criss-crossed by a number of narrow paths that led from bus stops to the road. If all roads once led to Rome, then here on the green all paths once led to a bus stop. In the middle was a series of holes that had been dug as dens by the kids from streets on both sides of the green. Yet even here in what seemed to the casual observer to be little more than a 'no man's land', an invisible border ran down the centre to segregate the rivals from the opposing streets, and anyone found on the wrong side of the green would suffer the fate of being pushed into a patch of nettles by a group of jeering boys. Sometimes there would be 'Viking style' raiding parties and any prisoners captured would undergo the nettle ritual. After the yelling and screaming had died away there would be a frantic search for the healing dock-leaf that helped to subdue the stinging pain of nettle rash. I have returned home many times with my legs pulsating red and covered in small white spots where the nettles have done what they do best. Fortunately we were all young, fit and agile which literally helped to keep us on our feet and able to brave any encounter with nettles, for to lose your balance as the enemy pushed you into the waving stinging menace would be very bad news indeed and not only would your legs get a good pricking but also your hands, ears and face that guaranteed to send you into convulsions of mind-numbing agony.

Beyond this waste land lay another which to make life simple we also called 'the green', except on this green not only did the paths through the undergrowth lead to a bus stop they also ran to a row of shops and a seedy block of lavatories that sat in the middle of the desolation. Again this area was not without its hazards. To circumnavigate it on the pavement meant that I had to pass a house that had been notably personalised by its owners in the form of a missing garden gate, a few twiggy remains of a once valiant privet hedge that seemed to have been in a war zone, a scattering of domestic rubbish in front of the house and at least two broken windows. There were always at least two broken windows which allowed anyone passing to hear the shouting of abuse from within. The occupants tended to be very vocal. It was a social experience unless you were a small boy like me who was quite likely to get thumped by a lad from the house for no other reason than the fact that he saw me passing and was much bigger than me. It was more likely to happen in the evening if I was sent to get some fish and chips. All you could buy at the chip shop in those days was battered cod, fish cakes, mushy peas and threepence or sixpence worth of chips all wrapped in good old well-fingered, unhygienic newspaper.

Alternatively, I could cross the green and run the risk of being set upon by a group of kids playing around the squalid lavatories. It could often be a mob of girls with mouths on them like fish wives and smelling not dissimilar as a result of playing all day in the lavatories. I have never understood what for generations of children, has been the attraction of playing in and around public lavatories where the flotsam and jetsam of the public relieve themselves of bodily waste before going on their way. Yet here in these vile temples devoted to the obnoxious smells, indescribable spillages and total misuse of toilet paper, young children are drawn like flies to a cow-pat to play, smoke an underage cigarette or indulge in an underage grope. Okay, so I admit to playing 'doctors and nurses' in my own outside lavatory but at least that was on home ground and in a rarely used private facility. I just never felt the need to go public, so to speak. Suddenly, everything appears to have turned a tad lavatorial. I think it must be time to take a deep breath, brace myself and with misgivings move up a notch to secondary school where the art of survival became almost a daily necessity. I might sometimes think I was safe, but for the main part it was merely an illusion. The bullies never missed an opportunity and eventually they would get you! The threat was always there, but you never knew just when they would strike.

6

The 'Rack' and other Torments

With a failed 11-plus examination under my belt I stood in line on the playground of Derwent senior school waiting once again to hear my name called out and discover in what class grade I was to be placed. The answer came and I was allocated to class 1B. I was obviously not clever enough to make the A grade. Must try harder. At the same time I was given a timetable telling me what lesson I should be in, what classroom number and what time I should be there. This was beginning to look horribly like the real thing. I felt somewhat unnerved that morning as the top classes of 16 year olds looked very big, very tough and very menacing. As the weeks went by they did not disappoint as they proved to us minors that they were indeed very big, very tough and very menacing. It did not take too long to discover that some of the teachers were equally as bad in their efforts to keep law and order in the classroom. The overall appearance of the school building was that of a prison for it was bleak brick and architecturally on a scale of one to 10 barely merited a one. It was two stories high with the girls occupying the upper floor and a playground that faced south overlooking a sort of school allotment. Very nice. We boys, on the other hand had the ground floor of the school with playgrounds tucked between three walls which for the most part shaded everything from the sun. I do not wish to make this sound like sour grapes, but while the girls looked sun-tanned and healthy enjoying the open space, we boys remained in the shade, pallid, unhealthy and barely free from mould on our weedy bodies. Around the side of the block where the two playgrounds met, segregation was maintained in the form of a white line painted on the tarmac which neither girls nor boys were allowed to cross. Even conversation was discouraged, but it failed to stop some of the older lads from fixing up dates with girls after school. Consequently, very little was seen of the girls and their existence came only in the sound of movement above us in the classroom along with the few occasions when we could ogle out of the window at their bare legs as they played netball in the playground. It often proved to be the only pleasant distraction during a day of academic intensity.

To me the lessons seemed harder than ever as well as having to cope with new ones like science and French and proper PE with fearsome looking equipment. Arithmetic suddenly became mathematics involving all manner of things that left my brain feeling addled and did I really care if Mr A left home at midday riding a bicycle travelling at 10 miles an hour towards a train travelling in the opposite direction at 60 miles an hour having left the station at 11.30am; and at what time did Mr B on board the train eating a ham roll and reading Tolstoy's *War and Peace* glance out of the carriage window and see Mr A speeding past on his bicycle? Well, to be absolutely honest, no, I did not care one iota and I suspect nobody else in the class gave a fig either, with the exception of the teacher who in my humble opinion should really have found something more useful to do with his time. There was history, but the least said about that the better. Geography I quite liked as it involved the country and other places in the world. I learnt things like England has a lot of long rivers, the Fens is really the sea bed, Wales has mountains and sheep and Scotland had bigger mountains and more sheep which is useful to the economy, for without sheep there would be no woolly jumpers and a serious absence of roast leg of lamb on the menu at Sunday lunchtime. Science lessons were a bit dry but were occasionally enlivened by somebody accidentally turning their Bunsen burner up too high and taking their eyebrows off.

Music lessons were a complete nightmare and the teacher Mr Goulder a competent psychopath. He continually waved his arms around in the air like a drowning man glaring at everyone through thick-lensed glasses that made his eyes appear maniacal in the extreme. His unbalanced behaviour was amply illustrated by his 'pièce de résistance' employed in his caning technique. His victim would be dragged out to the front of the class for whatever reason and Mr Goulder would bring down his cane on the finger tips so accurately that sometimes it would catch the nail and dislodge it, which as you can imagine was pretty painful. In this particular instance it was a bonus if you were of a nervous disposition and regularly bit your nails. After a term of Mr Goulder's music lessons, everyone was of a nervous disposition and bit their finger nails. Come to think of it I reckon it was Mr Goulder's sadistic caning that launched many of us into a habit that was hard to shake off. I bit my nails for decades afterwards and at one stage as a teenager my mother used to paint my finger ends with some truly dreadful gunk so if I stuck a finger in my mouth it tasted like a decomposing skunk. Well you get the point I am making never having actually stuck a decomposing skunk in my mouth.

Gymnastics replaced PE and we were made to perform in white shorts, vest and black pumps and forced to jump or crash over a vaulting horse, climb ropes, fall off or slip down and get some painful souvenir rope-burns. We also had to dangle forlornly off the wall bars like a row of badly hung washing uncertain of what to do next. In general we were a motley group of scrawny, badly coordinated kids who found it difficult to comply with the firm authority of the gymnasium, especially as most of us were more than capable of climbing trees, shinning over walls and leaping over fences of our own volition and enjoying the freedom that came with it. Having to do it to order seemed unnatural. However, to step out of line or not take the lesson seriously incurred the humiliation of being bent over a vaulting horse and having your behind whacked hard with the crepe sole of a plimsoll. This was not an edifying experience and thank goodness we were all too young to suffer from haemorrhoids. This punishment was normally meted out at the end of the lesson so that the pain of throbbing buttocks did not impede your ability, assuming you had any in the first place, to continue participating in athletic impossibilities; plus by the end of the lesson you would have been worked to the point of exhaustion as if you had done a 16-hour shift down a coal mine pushing fully laden trucks without so much as a single tea-break and no longer cared what happened to you.

Worse was yet to come if the teacher Mr Kensit decided we were in need of some fresh air. He would send us all off on a cross-country run that led across an immense area known as the race-course, along the black cinder track of the tip, hopefully avoiding stepping on a dead cat, then down by the pipe works and back over the race-course. This circular route was about 100 miles, or at least that is how it felt as I stomped along with my thin legs dangling out of my shorts alongside everyone else as we puffed, gasped, wheezed and panted, stopping with stitch, stopping with cramp or just falling over with fatigue and hoping death would put in a hasty appearance. The thing is that the entire route could be seen from the school where we knew Mr Kensit was sitting on the grass idly watching us all suffer and we all knew that he counted us back in like sheep, so there was no nipping off home instead of finishing the course. It often took a long time before every sweat-drenched, limp, soggy boy collapsed over the finishing line, rancid, worn out and drained of all desire to live, all that is except the winner Peter Bambury who always came first and actually enjoyed cross-country runs! After the trauma was over, waiting for me and a few pals was the hard slog home from school which was over a mile and all uphill. I just prayed there would be extra sausages for tea when I made it back. There normally was and left-over sausages lived on a plate in the larder to be snacked on by whoever fancied one. My mother, for reasons unknown, always wanted to know who had eaten them and when, as though she was some sort of Sausage-finder General during the Sausage Inquisition.

I first entered the French lesson with more than a degree of apprehension and somewhat confused as to why I should be made to learn another language particularly as neither of my parents spoke French, nor any of my relatives, in fact nobody I knew spoke any French at all, so if I learnt French who was there to talk to? At the time of course, I was too nervous and shy to proffer this as an excuse to not have to sit in class with everyone else chanting like clockwork automatons, 'notre, notre, nous, votre, votre, vous', and pointing a finger at 'le mur, la porte, ma tete, ma nez' and so on and so on. Then we would all take turn in shouting out our names like, 'Je m'appelle Bernard', or 'Je m'appelle Michael' which seemed a bit daft to me as we all knew our names anyway; and what with all that male and female stuff, well I found it all quite staggering. As far as I was concerned it might just as well have been a foreign language. Hmmm. The outcome from all this was that slow progress, terrible pronunciation and an inability to grasp anything much beyond the basics meant that most of us frequently felt the keen sting of the cane on our hands, or at least frequently enough to not compel us to want to learn French or have anything much to do with anything French. Perhaps on reflection I could say that it promoted, albeit subconsciously, the continued age-old disregard between the English and the French with the English still gloating to this day about how, despite being outnumbered by the French, we still gave them a damned good thrashing at Agincourt on a Friday they will not forget in a hurry. I reckon we organised the battle on a Friday so it would be over in time for the weekend and the chaps could get back home in time to cut the front lawn or do that bit of fancy thatch on the roof that the wife had been on about for ages. Sometimes I think it is quite incredulous how I can remember something like Agincourt nearly 600 years ago, not that I was there, but cannot for the life of me remember where I left my spectacles five minutes ago! Life has a habit of thrusting conundrums our way.

Avoiding the wrath of the teachers was one thing, but you also had to be on your guard against the antics of your classmates. For example there was a troublemaker called Ronnie Bembridge who enjoyed being an irritant if you had the misfortune, as I once did, to have to sit alongside him at a double desk. It was a writing lesson and everyone was hard at work with head bowed and tongue hanging from the corner of the mouth when Ronnie decided it would be highly amusing to nudge my arm and make me scrawl a line halfway across the page. Every time I started to write he would give my arm a nudge. After a few minutes of this I was getting very angry and very annoyed as well as being concerned about all the lines and smudges across my page. The teacher on his round of the classroom peering over everyone's shoulder finally arrived alongside me and peered over my shoulder. I guess he was not too pleased to see a page of writing looking more like an attempt at a Picasso and reacted accordingly. Before I knew what was happening I was out of my seat and in front of the class protesting. 'It wasn't me, Sir. Ronnie Bembridge kept nudging my arm.' 'Thwack', down came the cane across my hand. You see there really was no point in me trying to declare my innocence, because the teacher felt the need to punish somebody regardless of the facts, so 'thwack' the cane stung across my hand a second time and that was that.

There was, however, one incident when the table was turned on the teacher and it happened during a maths lesson with a teacher we all referred to as 'Buster', but not to his face of course. He was not a young man and sometimes seemed to be a little short on temper. He was also a little short in stature. A confrontation took place between Buster and a boy called Len who was a tall, well-built lad and had a natural leaning to being a thug. He could often be spotted roaming about the town centre on a Saturday with his gang of henchmen and if he spotted someone looking at their often noisy antics he would cross the road, stare you fully in the face and ask in an aggressive manner, 'Wot you lookin' at?' It was now that threats had moved up a few notches and 'bash your head in' and 'fat pig' had been replaced and the ubiquitous four letter 'F' word entered our vocabulary. Regardless of whatever reply you gave you still got a thump on the head. During this particular maths lesson an argument developed between the two of them. It resulted in a stand-off with 'Buster' becoming angrier by the minute, and Len becoming more and more defiant. Very soon 'Buster' lost it altogether and tried to drag Len out from behind his desk. Len being much bigger and a lot stronger pushed 'Buster' and sent him reeling backwards against his own desk whereupon he bombarded Len with a tirade of threats and all manner of punishments. As far as Len was concerned it was all water off a duck's back, so he picked up his chair and threw it at 'Buster' knocking him off his balance, stormed out of the room and presumably went home. We all sat completely mesmerised as 'Buster' with a visibly pulsating red head picked himself up, muttered something to us about getting on with some work and left the room. The entire class promptly erupted in an uproar as we all acted out with theatrical gestures our own embellished versions of Len versus Buster, versus the chair. It had all been a bit of a Wild West Show and despite the absence of any Indians it really had been 'Buster's last stand!' Len did eventually return to school but was always going to be problematic and I seem to recall a few years later while he was still a very young man that he had a terminal encounter with a passing car. And on that sombre note I will move on to the terror and the misery that often awaited us in the playground where it would have paid to be invisible, if only someone had discovered the technique.

A bell would sound throughout the school to announce the end of a lesson, and while it was often a welcome sound, especially if it was a music lesson and you had managed to complete the lesson with the same number of fingernails you had started with, it could also mark the beginning of playtime where you would be thrust out into the playground and find yourself at the mercy of the school bullies, of which there were many. By now all first year boys had seen the notorious and legendary 'rack' and we all knew that it was not a matter of 'if', but 'when' it would be your turn, and hiding in the lavatories for example could prove to be a grave mistake. Foolishly thinking that you would not be touched because you were using the urinal at the time was a serious blunder on your part, for the bullies would simply 'dead-leg' you behind the knee which propelled you forward into the dripping wet back of the lavatory and caused you to wee down your trouser leg. You were forced to live with the ignominy of wet pants, damp trousers and the pervading aroma of urine for the rest of the day. Even hiding in the cubicle itself did you no favours either for the bullies would hang over the door top, pelt you with lumps of sodden toilet paper and spit on you for good measure. Going to the lavatory during break time was frequently fraught with disaster and it was sometimes better to avoid it altogether and raise your hand in class in the hopes that the teacher would show mercy and release you from the agonies of a near bursting bladder. The drawback was that you would have to be very insistent by shouting 'Please Sir, I'm bursting, Please Sir I have to go, Please Sir' which invariably meant that upon your return you would be caned for not having gone at break time and also for disrupting the lesson. And so the 'rack' loomed ever closer until the day dawned when I was picked on to be one of the victims of the day. The 'rack' was merely a scaffold-sized pole that stuck out of a wall to which it was attached at both ends with a blade of metal at floor level. Its real purpose was that of a sizeable boot scraper. In the hands of the bullies this innocent looking boot scraper became an engine of excruciating torture more than worthy of being included along with 'things to do with Protestants on a wet afternoon during the Spanish Inquisition'. I was grabbed by two older boys and held with my back against the bar. My arms were then looped behind me over the bar and pulled hard from the front so the bar dug into my spine. This had the effect of trying to dislocate my shoulder joints and when my arms were thrust upwards at the front at the same time then this just compounded the pain as my elbow joints were then being stretched. I was utterly at their mercy for the harder they pulled the more the bar rammed against my spine and the more my joints were stretched. It was simple but effective and I consider myself to be lucky insomuch as I only suffered the experience once which was sufficient for me to carry the unforgettable and far from rose-tinted memory of that day throughout the rest of my life. It did cause me some lasting pain which made using my arms in class afterwards a little difficult especially when trying to hold a pen. Some unfortunates were picked on regularly and became frequent visitors to the 'rack' and it is little wonder that they did not resemble orang-utans with stretched arms dragging across the playground.

More perils stalked the playground at break time and avoiding the 'rack' did not mean you could prance about safe in the knowledge that it was someone else's turn to have the length of their arms increased because there were bullies elsewhere just waiting for the moment to strike. One such fate was to be dragged by two boys to a patch of sunlight, pushed to the ground on your back, whereupon one would kneel on your hands and the other sat on your chest and between them they would prise open your eye lids and make you look at the sun. Again, simple but effective as upon release all you would be able to see was a world of orange splodges passing before your eyes, which was somewhat of a handicap when the bell went and you had to find your way to the next classroom. Another practice that occurred almost on a daily basis was to be slammed hard against a wall by some big lad who then grabbed your testicles, or 'pills' as we called them, squeezing them hard enough to send you into a screaming fit as your eyes watered and the stabbing pain shot into your brain reducing you to a writhing, gibbering wreck. This was often followed by a coup de grace from your tormentor who would noisily fetch up a ghastly globule of phlegm and spit it at your face with unnerving accuracy. In fact, firing phlegm at each other seemed to be a general pastime at school.

It will now take only a little imagination to picture the sight that would have greeted the teachers when the bell rang announcing the return to the classroom. Staggering in through the door would be the latest victims of the 'rack', moaning and hunched with limp arms trailing by their sides. Other kids half blind would be wandering from side to side, clutching the walls of the corridor in the hopes of finding the right classroom door as they strived to peer beyond their world of orange splodges and flashes of light; and finally the poor unfortunates bent double, clutching their scrotums, whimpering or sobbing with streamers of sputum hanging from their face. I wonder what the teachers thought when they emerged from having a civilised cup of tea in the staff room to find themselves confronted by a rabble of straggling malfunctioning individuals. I suspect, if only for a fleeting moment that some of them wore that 'change of career' expression that I had witnessed in the past. Generally, they appeared to carry on as though everything was normal, and I suppose in a way, it was!

When the bell rang for lunchtime we were allowed to go home if it was conveniently near, stay for school dinner or just go wherever we wanted. Nobody seemed too bothered as long as we were back at school in time for the afternoon session. Quite often my friend Barry and I would take the short walk to Nottingham Road, a busy main thoroughfare filled with noise, fumes and dust caused by the almost constant traffic that rumbled to and from the town. Taking our lives in our hands we would run the gauntlet of lorries and buses to cross the road and flee to an alley between a cycle shop and the gable end wall of another building. This led onto a timeworn, humpbacked bridge over a disused canal. Along one side was a short row of terraced houses with rear gardens bordering the canal looking out to a scene of fields and hedgerows known to one and all as 'the meadows'. In essence it was a spread of countryside trapped between the hubbub of the main road and a distant complexity of railway sidings that echoed to the sound of shunting steam engines and clanking couplings. I sometimes used the sidings as an extended area of exploration by spending an afternoon clambering about the trucks and wagons hoping not to be spotted by anyone, then returning home rather dirty and smudged with oil. It was all harmless stuff compared to a lad in my class who a few years on borrowed a Diesel locomotive from the railway depot where he was an apprentice and drove it along the sidings to get home on a day when there was a national rail strike. I seem to recall that he managed to derail the engine whereupon he continued the rest of the way home on his bicycle. Given the fact he had stolen the Diesel it seems only sensible he should cycle the rest of the way home, after all it would have been a bit of a give-away parked in the street outside his house.

The meadows were criss-crossed by tracks and footpaths which at certain times of the day suddenly came alive by workers taking a short cut home. Shortly after the far off factory hooters had sounded the meadows would be invaded by an army of workers dressed more often than not in shabby faded raincoats and a war-time gas mask 'lunch bag' slung over one shoulder careering along the tracks at break-neck speeds on museum piece bicycles, yet showing great mastery of their machines when it came to negotiating the many sections of collapsed canal bank which they tackled with well-honed skills as would befit any dare-devil circus rider. In a field somewhere there was normally an encampment of swarthy gypsies with a collection of shiny caravans, mucky faced children and savage, barking mutinous dogs that fortunately were tied to trees, otherwise I suspect that had they been let loose they would kill on sight or tear the tyre from the front wheel of a passing cyclist before ravaging your ankles for dessert. As young boys we always passed the gypsy camp rather gingerly as they were regarded as fearsome places as indeed was the dark, shadowy coal yard beneath the railway bridge inhabited by burly men with very black faces and very white eyes. The scene here was made doubly scary by the bare bones of a sunken coal barge rearing up out of the black canal like the ribs of a long dead dinosaur. It was close by that for years two enormous cut-out men in white overalls marched across the meadows holding a ladder between them advertising Sisson's Paints. Despite their jolly appearance and determined gait, in all that time they never moved an inch so you would be in for a very long wait if you had booked them to come and paint your house!

An area of the meadows close to the town and near the slaughterhouse had a reputation for nefarious activities as a pub in the vicinity provided the pick-up point for an encounter with a lady of the night as well as being a convenient place to quench your thirst afterwards. Barry and I walked back through the meadows one evening after going to see one of Vivians Fuchs's Sno-Cats called *Haywire* that had played a vital role in his crossing of the Antarctic. It was a big orange coloured beast with cumbersome looking caterpillar tracks, but it held us in awe to think it had been at the bottom of the world. But our crossing of the meadows that evening was strangely spooky in the quiet twilight passing only two men and they, for some inexplicable reason, were standing motionless behind a hedge as we passed. Maybe they were murderers, or just really very good friends.

Meanwhile back at the canal bridge the pair of us would idle away our time sitting astride the broken lock gates gazing into the water looking for fish and diving beetles, or searching the adjacent hedge for bird's nests. Now what, you might wonder, could possibly interfere with the innocent activities of two young schoolboys enjoying the peace and calm exploring the banks of the canal? Well the answer to that question came in the shape of two young schoolgirls who were also interested in exploration, but exploration of an entirely different sort. We were lolling about on the lock side this particular lunchtime when they appeared alongside. After the usual conversational preliminaries were over the main instigator Vanessa Bass made her move by lying down on the grass with her legs wide apart and asking us whether or not we fancied her. If we did then we could meet her here after school and 'do her' as she put it, and to clear up any misunderstanding that might have occurred with the words 'do her' she pulled up her skirt and began to finger her knickers. 'I've bin done before, ya know' she boasted. 'I've bin done loads ov times by Dave Barnsley.' Dave Barnsley was a notorious school thug who would beat you up at the drop of a hat and was renowned for his seemingly endless supply of phlegm which could leave you in a grisly, slimy mess as you gasped for breath after he had punched you in the stomach several times. Vanessa obviously saw herself in the role of an irresistible temptress to any schoolboy or possibly a gangster's moll as she lay there exposing her knickers. Now I have to admit that at this point it all seemed to be going quite well and I was starting to lose interest in fishes and diving beetles until, that is, I looked more closely at her knickers. I should perhaps explain that this is a figure of speech and not to be interpreted as me actually moving in on my hands and knees for a closer look at her knickers. Call me old fashioned if you like, but believe me if you are confronted by the sight of a pair of knickers that have the look about them of a used dish cloth and strongly suggesting that she had indeed been 'done' several times, in fact to the point of being 'over done' then any further enticement will ebb quicker than an outgoing tide. There was also the fact that I was still a little unclear as to what 'doing her' actually entailed.

My hesitation and Barry's lack of interest in the soiled goods on offer somewhat took the wind out of her sails and she stood up, adjusted her skirt and walked off in a huff. We went looking for birds' nests. I feel at this point that you may be forgiven for thinking that I was developing into a sexual retard, but I would like to say in my defence that the incident involving Pamela Turnley's knickers and her 'thingy' was still quite fresh in my mind and I did not wish to find myself in the headmaster's office at the senior school being accused of fumbling in Vanessa Bass's knickers when all I was doing was looking for a bird's nest. You see my point? I was already forming the opinion that anything to do with a girl's 'thingy' was probably going to lead to trouble and as I discovered in later life that was pretty much the case. Remaining cautious did lose me the opportunity to go with some other lads to the back of my old school of an evening where apparently Celia Thompson would open her blouse and allow you to squeeze her blossoming breasts which was by anybody's standards extremely accommodating of her. However, there seemed to have been an underlying entrepreneurial motive for she charged you sixpence for 'titting her up' as it was called and sixpence could buy you a few sherbet lollies in those days. I decided to settle for the sherbet lollies for I reckoned that sucking on these could not get me into trouble. They failed to satisfy the curiosity of feeling Celia Thompson's young breasts, but again I have since found that life has often presented me with missed opportunities.

The one evening I did go to the back of the school was when a crowd had gathered but not to experience Celia Thompson's assets, but to witness the finale of *Sputnik 2* re-entering the earth's atmosphere. As it burnt up in the night sky leaving a trail behind it there were numerous sighs and comments about it being so sad, and such a shame because the Russian spacecraft was carrying on board a small dog called Laika who was being barbecued alive before our very eyes. Many years passed before the Russians finally admitted that despite Laika having orbited the earth for several weeks, the dog had in fact died of overheating in the capsule after only a few hours into the trip. Now whether this event proved to be more interesting than young lads orbiting Celia Thompson's breasts with their hands is a matter for conjecture, yet I cannot help wondering, where are you now Celia Thompson?

In case I am giving the wrong impression life at senior school was not all sex and violence. Well, actually for my part there had not been any sex, just violence. There were other things to get involved in like the after school film club which I only managed to attend once because you had to pay a few pennies to get in and I rarely had a few pennies. This is because there were two tuck shops on my mile long route to school so consequently any spare pennies got spent on sherbet lollies, flying saucers, or a frozen orange Jubbly. Sometimes it was simply wasted in a slot machine that dispensed tasteless, tooth-breaking gob-stoppers of planetary proportions and a tiny plastic skeleton if I was lucky. When you think about it there is very little you can do with a small plastic skeleton. It is certainly not going to frighten anyone. Both shops did a tremendous trade from the passing schoolchildren and probably went bankrupt when the school closed down some years later. The one film that I did manage to see was *The Cruel Sea* starring Jack Hawkins battling it out against German U-boats while on convoy duty in the north Atlantic. It was a stirring film with people in duffle coats getting very wet and being jolly 'stiff upper lip' about imminent danger. After the film show a group of us wandered back home through the streets and alleyways bursting with patriotism and shooting at anything and everything that we thought might be a German U-boat. We certainly put the wind up a few cats that evening.

Actually going to a proper cinema with my family, and there were many to choose from, was a rare and real treat. The nearest to me was the very 'art-deco' Majestic which was in walking distance from home. We never visited the many cinemas in town despite Mr Gilby being the manager of one. Mr Gilby lived at the end of my street but he never gave away any free tickets. He was in charge of the Black Prince cinema and drove a black van sporting the prince's black helmet on the roof. For ages we kids thought it really was the Black Prince's actual helmet, but now of course I know better. The thing is that at the battle of Crecy in 1346 the Black Prince was only 16 and therefore too young to hold a driving licence and the idea of him driving into the fray and defeating the French in Mr Gilby's black Austin A30 van does not settle easily in my mind. The first film I saw after watching the Pathe News, the Pearl and Dean advertisements and another telling us that ice-cream and Kiora orange was on sale in the cinema foyer was *The Red Berets,* which as far as I can recall was about a lot of blokes and Alan Ladd running about in red berets shooting at Germans after which they all went home. Then I watched *The African Queen* a film that has since become a cinematographic classic starring a rough, easy-going Humphrey Bogart, leeches and all alongside a prim and proper 'don't truck with me' Katharine Hepburn, both trying to dodge German bullets. Those Germans seemed to be everywhere. Walking back home afterwards in the dark I was convinced that German snipers were lurking behind every other privet hedge in those near pitch-black alleyways and I had nothing to defend myself with. I could not even counter attack with an empty Kiora orange drink carton. My parents could not afford to buy me such luxuries.

During my middle to late teens I had a friend whose mother worked as an usherette at the Regal cinema in East street and occasionally got free tickets for us to see a film. The very first film that I saw for free was the Gothic horror *Premature Burial* starring Ray Milland who for most of the film had his eyes popping out on stalks as though he had been plugged into the mains. While everyone was busy digging up graves and finding corpses with really bad fingernails through clawing at their own coffin lid, the haunting rendition of *Molly Malone* played in the background. After the frantic scramble to exit the auditorium before having to stand still for the playing of the *National Anthem* almost every person was either whistling, humming or singing 'She wheeled her wheelbarrow, through streets broad and narrow, crying cockles and mussels Alive, Alive-o' as they wandered away to their respective bus stops and not to the nearest cemetery. The other freebie I recall was that great film *Zulu* with its stirring opening score and a body count that far outweighed the full house that night. It roused within me an overwhelming sense of pride, patriotism and excitement as the Welsh soldiers sung their hearts out to *Men of Harlech* as Zulu assegais rained down upon them. At the height of the battle I had munched my way through two packets of popcorn. The defence of Rorke's Drift was heralded as the greatest moment in military history, although I cannot help but think that the hundreds of dead Zulu warriors might have viewed it differently and probably wished they had hung around after the massacre at Isandlwana before leaving to go home for tea and giving Rorke's Drift a miss altogether.

When I was still about 12 or 13 years old I went to the Saturday morning cinema club where after the show I would rummage through the bins behind the cinema searching for an occasional piece of discarded film clip. Saturdays also saw the advent of talent shows on stage at the Majestic where a ragbag assortment of kids with guitars, a tea chest and broom handle bass and a washboard and thimbles would bash out a searing rendition of the latest rock or skiffle song. These performances were usually accompanied by an onslaught of jeering, yelling and the sporadic missile after which we would all pile out onto the street, an unruly mob of scruffy kids wearing fluorescent green or orange socks, our only affordable contribution to the rock scene. It was the much older lads who wore the powder-blue Teddy boy suits with drainpipe trousers and spongy beetle crusher shoes that practised with a flick knife the mindless ritual of carving up the seats on the top deck of a bus. Teddy boys normally came with a built-in aggression factor that gave them the unquestionable right to smack you about the head if you so much as looked at them in the street. It seemed to be a period of my life that was continually spent ducking and diving to avoid trouble as much as possible in order to quite simply, stay alive!

Perhaps the high point of my time at the senior school was when the gym teacher, Mr Kensit announced that he was hoping to get together enough people to take on a week's adventure holiday in the Yorkshire Dales. We would be staying at Malham Youth Hostel and doing lots of walking, climbing and caving, so this was pretty exciting stuff and virtually unheard of in those days as a school trip. I had been doing this kind of thing with my parents on a Sunday for years, so I just had to be one of the participants. As a family we got by financially and somehow my parents managed to scrape together the money for me to go. I think it was mainly down to my mother who no doubt did some extra dressmaking for which she had an outstanding talent and was able to raise the extra cash. She was generally kept busy with this spare-time occupation and there seemed to be an almost endless stream of mothers and daughters calling at the house in the evening for a measuring or fitting session. At such times my father and I would be relegated to the kitchen out of the way in case the clients needed to remove some of their clothes which I thought a bit unfair as my sister was allowed to stay. I mean I would have been more than happy to just sit quietly reading my *Eagle* comic and not looking at girls in their underwear. Okay, so that is a complete lie, but I would only be seeking to further my limited knowledge of the secrets of the opposite sex. My mother would spend many evenings treadling like a determined Tour de France cyclist at her sewing machine, or circumnavigating the dining table drawing complicated lines on fabric with tailor's chalk before snipping at it with menacing looking pinking shears that resembled a shark's jaws with handles, and all the time muttering inaudible comments through a mouth bristling with dressmaker's pins.

Anyway, back at school preparations were going ahead for the trip and we were told that during the lunch break we had to practice abseiling. We were led by Mr Kensit through the forbidden territory of the upstairs girls' school and onto the flat roof of the school. A crowd of kids looking rather dwarfed had gathered in the playground far below to watch the fun (for fun, read, we hope somebody falls off and there is loads of blood and bones sticking out). Trying our hardest not to show any signs of fear we warily, one by one, walked backwards over the lip of the roof and descended with the aid of the rope. The method used was the old tried and tested classic abseil technique which entailed a rope passing over one shoulder and somehow wrapping around one leg. This screwed your trouser leg into a blood-stopping tourniquet around the thigh before commencing to saw your leg in two and any other bits and pieces in that area that might get caught up in the ruck of trouser and skin. After we had all performed a couple of descents we were heralded in the playground as rugged dare-devils, for we had all escaped death, no one fell off, and fortunately for all concerned nobody had been castrated. The onlookers probably felt a little cheated by this as they were really hoping that some ghastly happening would liven up an otherwise boring lunch break. However, as far as I was concerned the abseiling had become a turning point in my life for I had gone up onto the roof a mere schoolboy, but had descended as a man, a hero, a cut above the rest. This, of course was all in my head for I still continued to get spat on, thumped and kicked, but for my life at senior school it had been my finest hour.

The day of the trip eventually arrived and a disparate bunch of misfits wearing hob-nailed boots, baggy trousers tucked into socks, wind-cheaters with elasticated waist bands and an odd assortment of hats gathered on the platform of the railway station posing for the photographer from the *Evening Telegraph*. Did we look strapping, fearsome, hardy, or simply a gaggle of badly dressed kids looking faintly ridiculous? Only the photograph will tell and it is said that the camera never lies! After some hours on the train we regrouped on the platform at Skipton where we were told that a brisk walk along the river to Malham would, according to Mr Kensit be a good idea. Who else apart from Mr Kensit thought it was a good idea is unrecorded. It was a tad overcast when we set off to cover the 200 miles, or whatever it was to Malham with our rucksacks hanging off our backs. Apart from having to watch where we were walking we also had to listen to another teacher Mr Walters who gave a non-stop commentary on the flora and fauna of everything around us which was getting a bit tedious, until Mr Walters lost his balance and fell into the river which cheered us all up no end. While out walking a couple of days later Mr Walters delighted in showing us all a Curlew's nest he had found cleverly camouflaged against some dried grass. It was so cleverly camouflaged that Christopher Hancock who had not been paying attention, burst through the ranks to see what everyone was looking at and crushed one of the eggs beneath his boot. Mr Walters flew into a tantrum and swiped Christopher Hancock several times across his head, threatening him with a good thrashing when they got back to the hostel for being an 'idiotic, inattentive, clumsy-footed clod' who should have stayed at home. Christopher Hancock sulked for the rest of the day and was made to clean the hostel's lavatories for punishment.

It was an intensive week as we engaged in climbing Gordale Scar, walked to Malham Tarn, did a bit of scrambling and abseiling of the lower ends of Malham Cove and visited various caves including Bar Pot the back entrance to the awesome Gaping Ghyll. We were guided by some members of the Craven Potholing Club but were not allowed to descend the 100ft shaft. It would be many years later during half a lifetime of climbing and caving all over the UK and abroad before I had Bar Pot under my belt. Yet even deep in the heart of the Yorkshire Dales trouble sought me out as I, along with Tom Granger were reported by a younger member of the trip for frightening him with grisly tales of torture. We had made them up anyway seeing as neither of us had any experience in torture, not even in the school playground. We just had vivid imaginations. Unfortunately for us Mr Kensit did not appreciate our vivid imaginations and obviously thought that our minds needed to be occupied by more useful things, so he consigned us both to the kitchen of the YHA to peel a mountain of potatoes that were required for dinner that night. Neither of us was skilled at peeling potatoes due to the fact that we had never actually peeled a potato before and as the hours dragged on Tom became very bored, so he picked up a large handful of peelings and threw them across the table at me. This was extremely badly timed for at that precise moment Mr Kensit opened the door to see how we were getting on. He saw Tom wearing a look of surprise and me wearing some potato peelings. Mr Kensit did not seem at all interested in asking either of us for an explanation. We both got whacked on the backside with a plimsoll for messing about. Something drifted through my mind about 'It wasn't me, Sir' but I knew by then it would be a hollow plea so I simply accepted my punishment. Potato peelings aside, it was a fantastic week and we all lived off our 'gung-ho' tales for weeks afterwards in school.

During my second year at senior school I took the 13-plus examination which if you passed allowed you to go to a more technically orientated school or an art school depending on which section of the exam you had taken. Despite the mysterious disappearance of my crucifixion drawing some years ago I still persevered at home, painting dubious pictures in an effort to be as good as my mother who was a very competent watercolourist. My sister had already passed the exam a couple of years before and was ensconced at the art school. One morning during a science lesson I was ordered to the headmaster's office. This was always a terrifying prospect and as I walked along the corridor I racked my brains to think what trouble I might be in, but failed to come up with anything unless, of course, Vanessa Bass in a spiteful rage for being rejected at the canal bank had reported me with a concocted tale about an encounter with her grubby knickers. Much to my surprise the headmaster was all smiles and congratulated me on passing my 13-plus exam and that I would be leaving school at the end of summer term to attend the art school. So, I could paint after all! I returned to the science lesson and had to explain my absence to Mr Ewen who did not congratulate me on my success, but instead made some sarcastic comment about not knowing how I managed it. The thing is Mr Ewen never really liked me because I did not pay attention during his lessons and he had caught me one lunch break in the science room with my friend Barry playing with the terminal leads of a car battery. It made lots of loud threatening crackling noises and produced showers of sparks. Mr Ewen also made lots of loud threatening noises, but failed to produce any sparks.

I went home after school that day feeling immensely proud of myself. When I told my mother she was extremely delighted. My father was also extremely delighted. My sister, however, announced that after two years at the art school she was going to leave. Surely she was not harbouring a grudge after all these years because I had hogged all the red and blue wood blocks when we were very young,…or was she? After all there had been the business of her pouring my dinner over my head and a decade or so later she did slam the bedroom door on my thumb after a squabble over a hot water bottle. On the face of it I reckon I was more than justified in developing a persecution complex. She did leave the art school and got a job spending her wages and her spare time learning to dance at the Victor Sylvester ballroom, not that Victor ever appeared, bopping the night away at the Trocadero and snogging boys. For me it was a case of forever onwards and upwards as there was much to be achieved in my life and I was keen to get on with it.

7

THE WORLD'S FIRST QUASIMODO RABBIT!

L ife on the home front in the ensuing years changed noticeably as I gained a sense of independence and dabbled in a diversity of interests. I was becoming particularly appreciative of music despite having failed at school to master the recorder, if indeed such a thing is possible. As it is generally regarded as the most hated of instruments and consequently I may have been hated for playing it, then I can only conclude that it was fortuitous I was unable to make any other sounds on it that did not resemble a cuckoo with laryngitis. At home the wireless with its strange assortment of red glowing, dust covered valves remained switched on for much of the time and consequently I was brought up with programmes like *Friday Night is Music Night* and the toe-curling *Sing Something Simple*. Sunday lunchtime I listened to the eclectic collection of music on *Family Favourites* with Jean Metcalfe. I do not mean I listened with Jean Metcalfe in our living room. She was the one on the radio. The final piece of music was invariably classical and more often than not, Tchaikovsky's *1812 Overture* or Mendelssohn's *Fingal's Cave*. This would be introduced along the lines of, 'Gunner Rob Brierley serving in

Germany would like to say a big hello to his girlfriend Yvonne Braithwate from Oswaldtwistle who works as a pastry crust tester at the local meat pie factory. Rob sends all his love to you and says he can't wait to see you in September where he is looking forward to getting his teeth into one of your meat pies'. This was clearly an innuendo for Rob really saying that he could not wait to get home and give Yvonne a jolly good 'rogering', the point of Rob's intentions being dramatically illustrated by the salvo of cannons firing off in Tchaikovsky's finale.

Anyway, be that as it may I believe my first introduction to classical music came from being allowed to watch a programme with Brenda Huntley who lived down the street from me, because she had a television and let me watch it on rare occasions. The programme on children's television was called something like a *Cabin in the Clearing* which was about, well, a cabin in a clearing that became surrounded by scary, whooping red-Indians who shot flaming arrows at it and set the cabin on fire and that was pretty much that. But sometimes Brenda Huntley gave me a chocolate biscuit so that made it worth watching. However, the introductory music stayed in my mind and it was to be many years later before I discovered it was from Dvoraks *New World* symphony. Classical music followed me throughout my life and I clearly recall attending my very first live concert which took place in the chlorinated atmosphere of Queen Street swimming baths in town. To avoid any misunderstanding the bath had been boarded over for the occasion as otherwise treading water at the deep end throughout the entire concert would have detracted somewhat from the enjoyment of the music and made for an extremely exhausting evening. I remember the highly esteemed conductor clearly displaying his annoyance during a particularly quiet piece that was ruined by the bell of the nearby cathedral chiming out nine o'clock. At other times the intermittent swish and gurgle of a cistern being flushed in the gents' lavatories would filter into the music and give it that unexpected something. He was plainly not at all amused. This was definitely not the Royal Albert Hall.

I was once presented with an old wind-up His Master's Voice gramophone comprising of a massive cast-iron turntable covered in green felt and a contorted arm that closely resembled a section of chromium-plated colon with a needle stuck in the end. I use this analogy because I have since seen pictures of my own colon (without a needle stuck in the end) and the likeness is remarkable. Quite what I am supposed to do with the pictures the hospital gave me is questionable, after all they are not the sort of thing I would want to put in the family photograph album. Just imagine the scene on showing them to someone. 'This is me on the beach at Yarmouth, and this one is, well I never, a shot of my colon, and here I am again eating an ice-cream on the pier at Yarmouth, and oops! I don't know how that got in there but it's another picture of my colon.' I recently saw the images taken with a camera down a blocked-up drain and they also bore a remarkable resemblance to the inside of my colon. I think I had better return to the subject of the gramophone. With it came a record the size of a dustbin lid with the *Warsaw Concerto* on one side and a Chopin piano concerto on the other. Sadly due to there being a mouth-sized chunk missing from the edge of the record I never got to hear the beginning of either piece! Then someone unearthed another old record with a cheery little number that had a chorus line of, 'I would never, never go, all the way to Jericho, riding on a camel in the desert'. This also had a mouth-sized chunk missing from the edge.

I was beginning to be of the opinion that this was the only way records could be made and that I was never supposed to hear the opening section. That is until one day I discovered that Woolworths sold completely circular records that were cheap and affordable. Unfortunately they were cover versions of popular songs by obscure singers operating under the red Embassy label. This did not deter my father from getting in on the act by buying a version of *Old Cape Cod* by heaven knows who and boring my sister and I senseless by constantly playing the thing. We plotted to oust him off the turntable by going out and buying two proper records. My sister bought *All Shook Up* by Elvis Presley, and I bought *At the Hop* by Danny and the Juniors which was beaty but somewhat monotonous. And so war commenced as we all battled for a place at the gramophone until one day disaster struck during a playing of *All Shook Up*. We heard a loud clunking noise followed by a thud and Elvis groaned his way into a long, deep, drawn-out slur and the gramophone died. Elvis had unwittingly shaken the gramophone to a halt. My father took the thing apart and found the governor had broken. Due to the antiquated age of the machine he could only buy a set that turned out to be a tad too big, so that at every revolution of the spring box that drove the turntable the oversized governors hit a metal stud projecting from the box with a loud 'boing' which tended to take the edge of Elvis's shaking and Danny's hopping.

There was always plenty to listen to on the radio on a Saturday morning as we moved from skiffle with Johnny Duncan offering train time table advice about the *Last Train to San Fernando*, Nancy Whiskey having problems with a fast *Freight Train* and Lonnie Donegan's rambling and long-winded introduction as to the goings on of the *Rock Island Line* to the birth of rock and roll. This took the form of an apparently depressed Tommy Steele admitting that he never felt more like *Singing the Blues* and Bill Haley who for reasons best known to himself decided to *Rock Around the Clock* making a racket as he did so. From here on all hell broke loose and pop music took over the world.

The one thing I had not bargained for in the thick of all this was my next door neighbours, the Baldrys. Roy Baldry had purchased an electric record player with an apparently limitless volume knob and his bedroom was next to mine. I have to say that being subject to hours of hearing Elvis bawling out

Jailhouse Rock through the adjoining wall is not how I wished to spend my time in the sanctuary of my own bedroom. I found myself harbouring malicious thoughts about both Elvis Presley and Roy Baldry that terminated in death, and this as it transpired was only the tip of the iceberg. Mr Baldry owned a piano. You could stake your life on every piano session taking exactly the same format whereby he would start off slowly and then work himself up into an unhinged frenzy. This took the form of him completely desecrating a perfectly good tune by embellishing it with a seemingly uncontrollable onslaught of twiddly bits and complex flourishes that would suddenly stop dead. I assumed at this stage that Mr Baldry's fingers had tied themselves into such a ravel that Mrs Baldry would be summoned from her knitting to come and untie them, whereupon he would set forth again with admirable gusto until he had knotted his fingers together a second time. You might just be able to imagine the effect this had coming through the wall and invading the privacy of my home.

It was time for me to take revenge and I discovered purely by accident just such a way. On a Saturday afternoon Mr Baldry and his sons would be glued to their television screen watching a football match for they were devoted fans of the game and even dressed in their team colours while shouting and yelling at the set. Meanwhile I was upstairs in my room playing with my electric train set and by chance had stumbled across the fact that each time I ran an engine around the layout it produced a snow storm of epic proportions on their television screen. Now I had power quite literally at my fingertips. The Baldrys understandably became very irritated and more than a little miffed each time the players disappeared into a raging blizzard accompanied by ear-splitting hissing and crackling noises. This was great fun and it was quite some time before they tracked me down as the perpetrator and I learned that I needed some suppressors on the layout to eliminate the interference.

But things were about to become even worse. My father had read about a competition where you could write a song and compose a tune, and if you won it would be sung by Tony Brent or some such person. My father enthusiastically embarked upon writing the lyrics for a song he called *Sleepy Valley* and when it was finished he rushed around to Mr Baldry to see if he could compose a tune for it. I considered this to be a very serious error on the part of my father as Mr Baldry slowly, painfully and noisily set about his task. The house walls reverberated constantly and I took cover down the back of the settee with a cushion clamped over my head. The thing is, *Sleepy Valley* was a soulful little number that instantly lodged itself in my brain where day after day, week after week it gradually gnawed away at the few remaining shreds of sanity that I possessed until I felt that only death could be a sweet release, and I was not necessarily thinking solely of my own. Plinkety-plonk went the piano as my father sang out 'See you down in sleepy valley' while I gritted my teeth trying valiantly to stifle a desire to machine gun everyone to death in sleepy valley and slam the piano lid down hard on Mr Baldry's fingers. On and on it went, hour after hour, night after night through the walls of our living room until they decided they had had enough. For a musical finale Mr Baldry turned up the tempo a couple of notches by bashing out on the keys a jazzed-up rendering of 'I love to go a wandering, along a mountain track, and as I go I love to sing with a knapsack on my back'. Now for reasons unknown Mr Baldry's dog took exception to this song and howled loudly throughout like a tormented banshee, creating unbearable bedlam. It was quite apparent that this cacophony of dog and piano was divine retribution for me running my train set during their football matches. I had no alternative but to concede to defeat especially as my father had unashamedly joined ranks with the enemy by colluding with his *Sleepy Valley* masterpiece. By now I wished that Mr Baldry would actually go a wandering along a very precipitous mountain track with his knapsack on his back loaded with nitro-glycerine and fall off taking his dog with him. They would certainly go out with a bang. Luckily the budding Rogers and Hammerstein duo did not make the finals and both went back to their day jobs and the world as I knew it returned to normal.

I eventually sold my railway layout for the princely sum of seven pounds and embarked upon other interests. Now there can be very few people that have not at some time or another kept a pet dog, cat, mouse, rabbit, guinea pig or a host of other things that became a passing fancy like terrapins or stick insects. I cannot be alone in thinking that of all the pets normally found in households throughout the land, stick insects must rate as the most boring and inactive of them all. They are about as riveting as paint drying and are capable of mustering about as much enthusiasm as being told that you are to be shot at dawn. My uncle who lived opposite me was quite a keen amateur naturalist encouraging me to go for rather more interesting animals to keep as pets. He was also a keen angler and had an unhealthy habit while fishing of keeping maggots in his coat pocket and then forgetting about them. He would return home at the end of a day's fishing, hang his coat up by the kitchen stove where the maggots would turn into chrysalises and then into flies that invaded the room in droves. This did not please my aunt as she tried valiantly to prepare a meal amid a cloud of annoying, buzzing, black flies. My aunt was very long suffering. One time she had to share her kitchen work top with a tank containing an axolotl, a sort of halfway amphibian that comes from Mexico and has a feathery hair-cut and wears what seems to be a permanent smile on its face. It did very little apart from swim lazily inside its tank and grin inanely at you through the glass.

In a well-meaning gesture my uncle presented me with a large catfish in a heavy glass laboratory tank. The catfish was black, sleek and had a flattened head brimming with whiskers. My mother immediately took against it and placed it in the window at the back of the house saying it was quite horrible and what was wrong with having a pretty coloured goldfish like everyone else had. Well I did not want a pretty coloured goldfish like everyone else and was quite happy with my catfish which I imaginatively called Blacky. In truth I could see where she was coming from for as far as I know, no catfish ever won a prize for its good looks and mine was no exception. I feel sure that if it ever had the occasion to glance in a mirror it would have frightened itself! Over a period of time the sides of the tank became completely covered in algae and consequently, little was seen of Blacky for weeks at a time as he spent his days in his green world eating the offerings of fish food and doing whatever it is that catfish do all day in a tank full of pond weed. Now and then he would clear a patch of algae by pressing his whiskery face against the glass and peer at us having tea, a spectacle that always unnerved my mother as she was convinced Blacky was harbouring malicious thoughts because his tank was rarely cleaned out.

One dark wintery evening my mother came to close the curtains for the night and saw that Blacky was floating belly-up in his tank. He had finally passed on to that great fish tank up in the sky where all good catfish go; a paradise of warm clean water with an abundant supply of yummy ant eggs to feast on. However, a dilemma arose as to how to dispose of him, so she suggested that my father should flush old Blacky down the lavatory pan as a suitable watery finale. My father raised objections on the grounds that Blacky was far too large and would undoubtedly block the system, thus causing a great inconvenience particularly, I suspect, with regard to his own classified and top-secret sessions with the eucalyptus cream. With Blacky laid out in state on an old dinner plate my mother suddenly solved the problem by opening the window and tossing him into the back garden. I mourned the death of my catfish for about five minutes as he was not really the sort of pet

I could get close up and personal with. Algae always stood between us and hampered any kind of true relationship.

Next morning my mother drew back the curtains. There had been a mild overnight frost and there still lying on the soil, amazingly ignored by all the neighbourhood cats was the lifeless body of Blacky; lifeless that is, apart from the opening and closing of his mouth. He was either gasping his last, or as seems more likely, he was mouthing a profusion of derogatory expletives at my mother as he fixed her in his gaze with a beady eye. My mother stood transfixed with horror, disbelief and guilt as she stared at the sight that confronted her. She immediately dismissed from her mind all thoughts of her daily regime of a cup of tea followed by a bacon sandwich that until now only an atom bomb exploding in the living room would have caused her to change this routine and rushed outside with a bucket of water to salvage poor Blacky from a night to remember. She salted the water slightly to help heal the grazes that Blacky had incurred when he had landed badly on the ground, which is not surprising for Blacky had not been in the habit of hurling himself out of the window or anywhere else for that matter, so naturally he had not been able to put in any practice when it came to landings. The outcome from all this was that Blacky lived on for another couple of years before he finally curled up his fins for good and I replaced him with a snake.

Admittedly, it was only a harmless grass snake, but it was extremely adept at escaping and then hiding somewhere in the house. It was once discovered entwined decoratively around the poker by the fireside and another time curled around the moulded legs of a chaise-lounge. It was obviously a bit of a show-off. The thing is that each time it escaped and our neighbour Mrs Baldry found out, she would immediately barricade herself in her house and refuse to come out or even open the door to anyone. Her fear of snakes I fancy was a bit misplaced for it was after all, merely a grass snake and not a 30ft boa-constrictor that was going to slither through the letter box of her front door, eat her budgerigar and then crush the life out of Mrs Baldry. But there was no reasoning with her until the snake had been re-captured and was back in its tank where it would slide around plotting its next daring Houdini-style escape. Predictably, during one of its escapes it disappeared and I never saw it again, so I replaced it with a small alligator.

It was only a very young alligator but he was a surprisingly nippy fellow who could leg it around the living room floor at great speed and was often quite difficult to catch, especially as he owned two rows of needle sharp teeth that he would use without hesitation. He lived by the fireside in a glass tank to keep warm and I would feed him worms in the morning before I left for school. As he chomped his way through a mouthful of writhing, dangling worms, my mother sat at the other side of the fire chomping her way through a bacon sandwich. After only the first morning she rapidly came to the conclusion that the sight of wriggling part-masticated worms was a bit too grisly to watch during her breakfast, so from then on she threw a tea towel over the tank and ate in peace and out of sight of my alligator. I thought this was a little unfair, after all, my alligator was not put off his breakfast by the sight of my mother eating hers and even if he was put off he was in no position to throw a tea towel over her head. He mysteriously died after about three months and my theory is that after the business with the tea towel he developed an inferiority complex and could no longer cope with life. He knew he was not really liked, so I replaced him with two non-existent geese.

They should have been a pair of Canada geese. I say should have because they never actually materialised. It all started by me finding a beautiful coloured pheasant flapping about in the back porch one summer evening. I quickly constructed a run of wire-netting for it to live in and all was well until the neighbours complained about him honking at 4.30 in the morning when he was happily strutting around and shouting for his breakfast. It would appear that none of the neighbours wished to have breakfast at 4.30 in the morning, in fact none of them even wanted to be awake let alone get up at that time, so my pheasant's popularity was short lived and I had to let him go. It was not long before I had spotted a replacement on the lake of a public park. I wrote to the appropriate authority asking if I could keep two Canada geese in my back garden. They replied saying that they had no objections which I thought was jolly decent of them particularly as the two geese were going to be kidnapped from the park which they owned, but of course I did not mention that bit in my letter and they did not ask. I set my plan in motion. An American acquaintance of questionable character that I had met during a summer holiday job at a private zoo said he would do the kidnapping for me and deliver the pair of birds to my home. I waited and waited and waited in vain, the birds never turned up and neither did he. I found out later that he was doing a stint in prison. Perhaps he had been caught stealing two Canada geese from a public park. In all fairness, I was aware that he had been inside for some offence in the past, but he was a really likeable guy. Maybe he was just not too good at being a criminal. Anyway, I replaced my two non-existent geese with a vivarium that over a period of years housed tree frogs, poison frogs, lizards, a chameleon and my pride and joy a pair of large iguanas.

The two iguanas called Iggy and Uggy had a long and chequered life. After my time at college I moved to my first job in East Anglia and my iguanas came with me, or to be absolutely correct they came on their own by train. This does not mean that they lounged about in a first class compartment with a flask of tea and some banana sandwiches, but that they were dispatched in a large cardboard box spending the entire trip in darkness. I received a phone call from a nervous sounding man in the parcels office at Huntingdon railway station informing me that he had taken delivery of a box labelled 'LIVE

REPTILES' which in his opinion seemed to contain something that was very live and very restless and would I please take whatever it was away as soon as possible. I got the distinct impression that the poor chap feared for his life if they managed to break out of the box. It was only after I had taken them home and released then into a new vivarium I had built when I saw that Iggy's back was hunched and askew as if it was broken, yet he showed no signs of any kind of paralysis. It turned out that he was suffering from soft-bone caused by a deficiency in vitamin D. From then on I had to grab him daily to administer liquid vitamin D down his throat with the aid of an eye dropper. This never failed to get him in a bad mood. A colleague at work who was a pathologist took Iggy on an outing for the day to London and the Royal Veterinary College where he was heralded as a uniquely interesting specimen of soft-bone. Iggy was examined, x-rayed and paraded about before classes of students eventually returning home with a folio of photographs and a medical report. I noted under the section on behaviour that someone had written the words 'temperamental and unpredictable'. This was based on the fact that Iggy had bitten two of the students and drawn blood. He certainly made his mark that day.

Shortly after this episode I returned home one day to find that between them they had managed to push out the plate glass front of their home and were running freely about the house. As they are fairly fastidious animals I gave up and let them have the run of the house and it was always challenging to come home and find out if they were lounging on the stairs, sunbathing in the front window or draped along a book shelf. In truth it would have been more useful if I had returned home and found that they had cooked dinner for me, but it never seemed to enter their heads. They both became very sociable creatures with their new-found freedom and would climb onto the table most mealtimes to feed off the side of my plate, showing a great penchant for apple pie and custard! Their favourite food was really bananas and I was convinced they viewed almost everything as a banana especially fingers and on one occasion when I got within range, my nose, which bore two half circles of teeth marks for several days. Iggy finally died from his condition leaving Uggy to roam around on his own until the day came when he could no longer resist the call of the wild, so employing what can only have been an amazing acrobatic feat he somehow scaled the wall of the kitchen to a partly open window and disappeared into the great open world of the Fens. I never saw him again and for all I know all these decades on he may still be stomping through the fenlands of East Anglia, secretly causing mayhem as he lives out his life thinking that everything is probably a banana and should therefore, be attacked and eaten.

During my early teen years my father, a very erudite man, was taking himself off to various evening classes held at the Workers Education Association and studying all manner of subjects from geology to anthropology. The latter involved a lot of old bones and I took a peripheral interest to the extent that I desperately wanted to possess a human skull. I did a lot of asking around at the time but always met with the same excuse that everyone was using theirs and seemed reluctant to indulge me. I learned to settle for less, for sometimes less can mean more. More came one Sunday afternoon in the form of a rather large horse skull in the car boot of a friend of mine's parents. My friend said he had spotted it in the bed of a stream and thought I might like it. I, of course, was delighted and carried it into the house with glee. My parents looked on wearing expressions of resignation that seemed to say what was wrong with collecting stamps or matchbox labels instead of turning the house into an open cemetery? My friend's parents looked on wearing expressions of bewilderment and suspicion and refused to come in saying they were in a bit of a hurry when what they really meant was that if they entered the house they feared they might be added to my collection; and why was their son mixing with someone who had an obsession with skulls? I did not really care what anyone thought for it was a superb specimen and was large enough to make an unusual seat to sit on in my bedroom. I then began to wonder how I could further my collection when I suddenly remembered the slaughterhouse on the edge of the meadows. This was my next port of call.

Apart from the place smelling quite badly and always having blood running past piles of salt and out of the entrance into a drain in the street, it was not quite as gruesome as I thought it might be. I leaned my bicycle against a wall and entered the slaughterhouse and a world of clanking metal, carcasses swinging from giant hooks and a group of men wearing blood-stained aprons sitting around as though they were having a tea-break part way through a massacre. It was, in short, a charnel house of blood and cadavers waiting to be sliced open with razor sharp knives and chopped into pieces with menacing looking cleavers. Despite the overall sickening sights and smells in the place, the intimidating men wielding knives were very obliging to my request and presented me with a cow head in a particularly ghastly condition as its horns had been sawn off, but it still retained a tongue and two eyeballs hanging from their sockets. This was going to need some serious work on it. He thoughtfully wrapped the bloodied skull in a couple of sheets of newspaper, whereupon I balanced it on the handlebars of my bicycle and set out for home. All was going well until I joined the busy stream of traffic flowing out of town, for it was late afternoon and masses of people had finished work and were, like me, heading home. Fate of course waits for such opportunities and conditions like this and that afternoon it saw me coming. I was labouring uphill from a steep sided dip beneath the 'BASS' railway bridge as it was always known, standing up on the pedals waving from side to side as you do when fate struck. I had just made the top of the incline and was passing a line of young ladies standing in a bus queue who worked in the nearby offices of the pipe works when the head dislodged itself from the handlebars and hit the road with a dull thud. I stopped after a couple of yards and looked back to be confronted by a truly hideous spectacle. The newspaper wet with blood had flapped off revealing the severed head lying on the road in front of the bus queue with both eyes dangling from their sockets and a massive grey tongue lolling out of a mouthful of grinning teeth. Almost in unison a gasp came forth from the office workers along with cries of 'Oh my God, what on earth is that' and 'That's revolting, I think I'm going to throw up'. As cars and lorries swerved to miss the grisly skull I felt the bus queue were of the opinion that I had murdered and decapitated someone or something and must therefore be a psychopathic maniac who should be avoided at all cost and promptly locked up. I base this assumption on the fact that as I walked back to collect the skull, not a little embarrassed and red in the face, no one offered to give me a hand. In fact most of them were still holding their hands over their mouths glaring at me either with fear or disbelief as I quickly retrieved the skull before I added to the roadside gore by becoming a traffic accident statistic. I could still sense all those eyes burning into the back of my head as I rode away with my specimen now looking a little worse for wear not that it had looked in perfect health prior to the mishap.

When I arrived home my mother did not appear to share my enthusiasm especially when I suggested that perhaps I could boil the head on her cooker in an old tin bath to make removing the fleshy bits easier. She refused to have it in the house and I was banished outside to pick away at it in the back garden. The eyes proved to be irremovable and were presumably attached to the skull with hawser cable and the tongue was not much better but did eventually come out after a lot of yanking and hacking at it with a kitchen knife. But overall it was still pretty messy and I was rapidly losing heart. In desperation I threw it onto the shed roof where over a period of six months or so, plus a contribution by some starlings and a few hundred maggots it was picked fairly clean, but not before my father had threatened me several times to get rid of it. The problem was that the bathroom window was directly over the shed roof and when he had occasion to relax in the bath on a summer evening with the window open it seemed that a few dozen flies left off feasting on the remaining putrid meat to zoom through the window and join him not only in the bathroom but sometimes in the bath as well. My father was not a man who invited companionship in the bath and certainly not black, buzzing, irritating, germ-ridden house flies that drove him to distraction and forced him to leap around swiping wildly at them with a loofah. I could see as bathtime sessions go this would not be called relaxing. The outcome of this saga is that the cow skull did finally join the horse skull in my bedroom where they stayed for many years until much later in life when feeling it was time to part with them I donated the pair to the biology room at Hinchingbrooke Grammar school where for all I know they languish to this day.

Now it was time for something completely different and far more challenging as my quest for knowledge and a desire to be involved with something different led my curiosity into the strange world of taxidermy. My paternal granny had presented me one day with what had once been my father's pet guinea pig as a boy. Seemingly on a whim she had decided to have it stuffed and cased by a taxidermist that used to have a shop on London Road which I think I vaguely remember. Anyway, the guinea pig called 'Tiggy' apparently had the run of both house and garden but one day found its way into a patch of cucumbers. Here it met a sad fate by gorging itself to death probably leaving this world with one final loud explosive belch. Tiggy still lives with me to this day in body, albeit stuffed, if not in soul. I developed a burning desire to stuff anything dead I could get my hands on fired by a book I had borrowed from the town library entitled *The Art of Taxidermy and Museum Display*. It explained everything from how to stuff a small bird to digging out the insides of an elephant. I was hooked. Once again my mother had that familiar look of hopeless resignation on her face about my latest venture. She was particularly emphatic that under no circumstances was I ever going to shovel out the insides of an elephant in her kitchen, as apart from the mess it would make it would also interfere with her preparing my father's dinner when he got home from work. 'You know' she said sternly as if trying to discourage me, 'how tetchy your father gets if his dinner isn't ready when he walks through the door'. In my defence I assured her that the chances of finding an elephant lying dead on the pavement outside in the street were pretty remote and anyway it would never fit through the kitchen door.

All I was lacking for my first attempt was a dead body. I eyed-up the neighbourhood cats, next door's dog and a small boy who lived at the other end of my street called Tony who was a bit daft and would probably not realised he had been stuffed. In the end I settled for a safer option and went fishing and caught a roach. I took it home, gutted and skinned it on an enamel-topped table that my mother had reluctantly surrendered for my macabre activities then filled the empty body with silver sand. When the body had hardened I emptied out the sand, mounted my fish in a case I had made, labelled it professionally with adhesive lettering 'Common Roach. *Rutilus rutilus*' (I knew you would be impressed by that bit of Latin) and hung it on the wall above my bed. As I lay in bed that night I was filled with a great sense of achievement. The other thing was that as I lay in bed that night my nostrils became filled with a vague smell of fish. By the third night there was a very distinct aroma that conjured in my mind the image of a neglected corner of Billingsgate fish market. Something had gone wrong. Originally skins were prepared with arsenic, but my local chemist, rather unreasonably I thought, refused to sell me any as according to him the finger of suspicion would automatically point at me if a sudden decline in the population of my immediate neighbourhood should occur, so instead I had to settle for alum. My mother said the smell was definitely unhealthy and would make everything else in the house smell of rotting fish. My father told me to get rid of it as it would attract a plague of flies and he was not financially placed as to be able to wander around the house chain-smoking Woodbines to rid the rooms of flies. The roach was consigned to the dustbin.

Undaunted, I began to plan my next move when fate intervened by presenting me with a bat that had mysteriously died in the back porch. This on the surface seemed a lot easier than the fish as it was nothing more than a furry blob with wings. Try as I might I could not get its wings to stay up and it just kept on looking as if it was having a bad wing day. I put it in my special 'Specimen' cupboard which contained an eclectic collection of bits of bone, feathers, bird's eggs, butterflies, moths, a gigantic scary house spider and the curled nail from my big toe that had come off in bed one night for reasons best known to itself. I continued to find dead things and spent hours gutting and hacking away on the table in the kitchen with my long suffering mother who, for the most part, kept her back turned on my new hobby in which I was having limited success. My stuffed house sparrow seemed to be permanently drunk and kept falling over and a pet guinea pig I stuffed resembled a Yule log with a leg at each corner, but my finest hour was yet to come.

One day I received a message saying that my great grandmother's budgerigar had died and could I stuff it for her as she was immensely fond of her pet and would still like to have it around her. My fame had spread for she lived on the other side of town a bus ride and then a trolley bus ride away. She lived in a row of terraced houses that terminated in a vinegar factory at the bottom of the street. The acrid pong of vinegar fumes in the air served as an early warning that the trolley bus was approaching her stop. My great granny had always seemed ancient to me and incapacitated to the extent that she lived and slept in a cluttered downstairs front room of her house along with her beloved budgerigar Joey. I always remember on the few times we visited her being intrigued by a large lump that stuck out from her neck and which in my young mind had the exact proportions of those tinned steamed puddings you could buy, which is what I thought it was. I thought that somehow she had been unable to swallow it whole and it had become lodged in her neck. On the face of it, swallowing a steamed pudding whole would have been a challenge to anyone but that never occurred to me at the time. It was years before I was told it was a goitre.

Anyway, great granny would lie propped up in her bed croaking away at Joey subjecting him to a constant barrage of, 'Hello Joey, hello Joey. Who's a pretty boy eh? Joey's a pretty boy aren't you Joey? Yes you are Joey, yes you are, Joey's a pretty boy'. Whether or not Joey thought he was a pretty boy will never be known because Joey never answered back, but I reckon that Joey got so utterly hacked off with this continuous bombardment that he committed suicide in his cage with a piece of cuttle-fish bone having decided that death would be a welcome release from the daily 'who's a pretty boy' interrogation. Joey arrived in a box and when I removed the lid my jaw hit the floor for between his legs was a featherless bald bulge the size of a ping-pong ball. Joey was not a pretty boy. I suppose it had been some sort of tumour but what on earth was I going to do with Joey with that thing hanging down between his legs? Not surprisingly my bible *The Art of Taxidermy and Museum Display* did not have a section dealing with skin-covered bulges between the legs of dead budgerigars so I was at a bit of a loss as to my next move. However, needs must, so after stuffing Joey's body I pulled the naked skin flap up and under one wing where I sewed it in place out of sight. Joey was then displayed in a glass-fronted box so his bad side could not be seen, otherwise I am afraid that no matter how you viewed poor Joey he did look as if he was carrying a small brief case under one wing. The end of the tale is that great granny was apparently very happy with her restored Joey. I just hope that she did not continue telling dead Joey just what a pretty boy he was, as I for one knew that he was far from being a pretty boy. My greatest challenge was waiting for me just around the corner and would subsequently prove to be the defining point of my doomed attempts at taxidermy.

There was a 14-year-old girl called Amanda, some three years younger than me who had developed a bit of a crush and was forever bringing things around to my house for me to look at as an excuse to see me. I suppose I was flattered particularly as the young Amanda was developing some very desirable shapes that I feel sure she would have been willing to show me if I had asked her. I base this assumption on the fact that whenever she spoke to me she cocked her head to one side, looked at me with soft, dewy eyes and asked me through pouting lips if I knew anything about whatever it was that she was holding in her outstretched hand at the time. Amanda's visits became so frequent that my mother felt it necessary to inform me that she was an underage schoolgirl and that I should confine myself to her enquiries only. I wonder what she was getting at? Surely she did not think that I was going to stuff Amanda? One afternoon Amanda appeared at my backdoor looking rather upset and cradling to her blossoming bosom a large brown rabbit that had, until quite recently been her pet but which now seemed to be quite lifeless. Predictably she asked the question, did I know what was wrong with her pet rabbit? Well the fact that it was cold, stiff and not breathing was a clue that strongly suggested it was dead. Feeling pretty confident about my on the spot diagnosis I broke the news to her. Amanda then wanted to know how it came to be dead.

I said I would look into it. I retired to the kitchen table and opened up the corpse. Because the rabbit had been dead for some time the blood was fairly congealed so my skilled professional diagnosis was that the rabbit had died of a blood clot in the heart. I think that went quite well and I even impressed myself. When I explained this to Amanda on her next visit she was obviously completely bowled over by my veterinary skills and squirmed with admiration, oozing sensuality from every pore of her young body. I could feel uncontrollable desire welling up inside me. I suspect Amanda could see for herself my desire welling up inside me. For a brief moment in time everything quite literally hung in the balance until the silence was broken by my mother shouting to me that dinner was ready and to come right away before my sausages got cold. Amanda and I parted for I am sure that even Amanda, young as she was, knew that a cold sausage was a most unsatisfactory affair. Amanda left saying I could do whatever I wanted with her furry brown rabbit. I immediately put in an order to a taxidermy supplier for two glass rabbit's eyes and got to work on my biggest project to date. I cut, and skinned, and scraped and poked about for hour after hour, then day after day making a wire frame from old coat hangers before I finally stuffed the rabbit and sewed it back together. My aim was to create a rabbit sitting upright with its ears cocked and looking alert. In reality I was left with a rabbit whose ears stuck out sideways like aircraft wings and kept leaning to one side, and to cap it all it had developed a mysterious hunched back.

I had to admit to myself there and then, that this was one of those defining moments in life that never really leaves you. I had unintentionally created the world's first Quasimodo rabbit. My hapless, hunchbacked Quasimodo rabbit refused to do anything that might suggest that once he had been a real rabbit and had not always looked like this. I could not get rid of his hump and somehow even his glass eyes reflected a dull glaze of resignation giving him an overall expression that intimated I owed him an explanation, or possibly an apology. I huffed, and sighed, and struggled to make Quasimodo look like a rabbit but he was having none of it. Despite my best efforts Quasimodo continued to look like a bad accident. My mother glanced over her shoulder and tittered to herself thinking I could not hear her above the sizzling of the chip pan, but I could and I knew she recognised a bad accident when she saw one. At this point I gave up and took the wretched rabbit to the outside lavatory where I left him with his front legs splayed apart, his ears sticking out at right angles and leaning to one side propped up on the lavatory seat. I could not quite bring myself to part so easily with Amanda's furry brown rabbit (could any man?) and my own stoic efforts to stuff the thing. Time passed and eventually my mother informed me that as the housing inspector was due for her annual visit, it might be prudent to remove Quasimodo from the outside lavatory for if she opened the door and found herself confronted by such an unexpected and bizarre sight we may very well have to bring her round by throwing a bucket of water over her head, or worse have to summon an ambulance. The humiliation of Amanda's rabbit ended with me dropping him into the dustbin and that signalled the finish of my short life as an inadequate but persistent taxidermist, and anyway I had an essay to write for the English teacher on my favourite animal and Quasimodo did not even get a mention. I apologise to Amanda for the ignominious fate of her brown, furry rabbit and pose the question, I wonder where you are now Amanda?

8

A Biology Mistress and her Bones

And so I come to the final round of my school life at a new school, beginning a new term, with new friendships to forge and a new uniform including a two-toned, blue striped wrap that until then was only worn by college students. We were indeed elitists and individuals and how different life was to become for me behind the almost hallowed portals of artistic endeavours which might just be the making of me. I used the word almost because the fact was that the columnar portico and entrance steps were somewhat diminished as above them a large edifice in stone announced that this once imposing entrance had been for the WATERWORKS OFFICES and not for an ancient and much respected institute of art that turned out Turners, Gainsboroughs and Rossettis on an annual basis. A more modest signboard to the side proclaimed the building to be a secondary school of art named after Joseph Wright of Derby. He was famously associated for his incredibly skilled paintings of contrasting light and shade (chiascuro effect) so brilliantly executed in paintings like *A Philosopher lecturing on the Orrery*, *The Blacksmiths Shop* and *The Alchymist*. Wright died in 1797 a few days short of becoming 63 and two years away from becoming a pensioner if there had been such a thing in his day. He was buried in St Alkmund's churchyard, a secret corner of the town locked in time where on a dark wintery evening the street lamps would cast a glow on a very tangible Georgian world of crumbling closely packed buildings and shadowy recesses. Sadly this wonderful atmospheric and historical remnant of Georgian Derby was sentenced to demolition in 1968 by a complete clown who should have known better, just to make way for a new road system. I only mention these facts because during my time at the art school I knew very little, if anything concerning Derby's best known artist. We were never for example taken to the art gallery in the town to view his works, or even taken to see his tomb prior to it being dug up of course, for to visit that spot now would almost certainly end with you being pancaked into the tarmac by the constant onslaught of traffic.

There was a similar lack of knowledge regarding the two school teams, Turner and Ruskin. Turner I knew was a painter, but Ruskin was best known as an art critic for he did little in the way of painting, so why him? Why not Gainsborough, or Constable or some other equally well known artist? Why was I confronted with so much confusion from the start, or had I just not been paying attention? Anyway, the old church square reminds me that there was once a shop there selling antiques and curios where I once paid the sum of twelve shillings and sixpence for a mounted pair of African cattle horns which I hung on my bedroom wall along with all my other trophies giving the impression that my room was in reality an annexe of the Natural History Museum in London. My mother said the room was a death trap with all the electric wires and sticky-tape joints that snaked under the carpet to illuminate all the display cases I had built full of stuffed animals. My father was in agreement with my mother and needed no further proof after I caused a short circuit one evening and plunged the house into darkness. The situation was compounded by the fact that at that precise moment he was very involved in singing something simple along with the radio programme *Sing Something Simple* and suddenly found himself singing something simple unaccompanied and in the dark. He bellowed some profanity from the bottom of the stairs and made for the fuse box to restore both the light and his musical indulgence. I nearly went without supper that night so heinous was my crime.

Anyway, back with the art school. The building stood a little out of the town centre and next door to the Ritz cinema and woe betide anyone caught by a teacher ogling the photographs on display of a raunchy film that was being screened. Opposite the school was the Grand Theatre where among other notable celebrities Gracie Fields had once belted out, 'Sally, Sally, pride of our alley' in that grating Lancashire voice of hers. The place was eventually transformed into the Trocadero and people bopped away the night to pop music and coloured lights. Around the corner was the Hippodrome and a little further on the town's only shop selling pornographic literature, so there was plenty to educate our young inquisitive minds during the lunch hour. It was a strange environment in which to find myself after my previous school life in suburbia. As pupils we were only allowed to enter the school from the street via a side gate that opened into a cobbled yard with a bicycle shed along one wall and the school building with its side entrance on the other. This yard hemmed in on all sides was not unlike a prison exercise yard and here at break times we were allowed out for a leg stretch and a breath of polluted town air. We made do with what little freedom it offered but were not forced to shuffle around in a circle under the watchful eyes of machine gun toting sentries, although the staff room did overlook the yard so there was a similarity.

Inside, the building stretched away with classrooms along the side and ending in a single storey annexe. About halfway along was a porter's lodge that was a glass windowed affair resembling a misplaced signal box and was the domain of Tommy Delton the school porter who had the unenviable job of attempting to maintain some form of discipline over the rowdy comings and goings of the pupils. I think he must have had other duties to perform, but whatever they were remained a mystery. In truth he was not really suited for the task of a disciplinarian because as a child my mother remembered being at school with him and she told me he was always called a sissy by the other boys, or a 'big girls blouse' as she put it, because he preferred to play with the girls. He did become the butt of many jokes and pranks, but in my later years at the school I got on quite well with him to the extent that he would loan me an occasional record which helped to further my growing interest in classical music. By then I was the proud owner of a Grundig tape recorder that had sufficient volume to almost drown out Mr Baldry's tangled piano playing and his son's back-to-back sessions of *Telstar* on his record player. By the main front entrance to the school an impressive staircase rose to the upper floor where more classrooms led off the main landing along with the school's antiquated lavatories and washroom that had an air of neglect about them. The classrooms had tall windows and high ceilings with some rooms having stately fireplaces made of fossiliferous marble which being a collector of such things (fossils that is, not fireplaces) tended to hold my attention and all the imbedded bi-valves and crinoids were far more interesting to me than boring old algebra, square roots and logarithms. Such things normally went well over my head and left my brain in a dazed and partly comatose state.

At the far end of the top corridor past the headmaster's office was the geography room that housed within one wall a sizeable walk-in safe. This was a left over from the days when the art school, aka waterworks office became an office for the Inland Revenue. Usually the safe stored school materials and sports gear, but sometimes we used it for storing an unfortunate victim who would be locked inside just prior to the beginning of a lesson, so that when his name was called out during registration only a muffled reply could be heard through the small air grill in the wall. This created much amusement for the rest of the class but not always for the teacher. If the teacher known to us all as 'Spider' was in charge then he would fling open the door and haul out the red-faced boy and give him nothing more than a telling off. However, if it was the headmaster Mr Buller who took over the lesson at the last minute then it would be preferable to keep quiet and sit out the lesson hopefully undiscovered, or if possible try to quietly commit suicide with a cricket bat and hope to complete the deed before being found out for Mr Buller was a fearsome figure and a man not to be trifled with.

I once remember Mr Buller recounting the story of how a man at some time in the past had rushed into his office still under the impression that the place was the Tax Office, dumped a couple of bags of money down on his desk saying everything was in order and apologised for not being able to stay because he really was in a terrible hurry and disappeared out of the door. Mr Buller did eventually trace the man and the money was returned. Whereas what he should have done was seize the opportunity and spend the money on a long weekend of wine and women on the beach at Acapulco. I recall one of the few times I had a confrontation with the dreaded Mr Buller that involved me being singled out during assembly one morning. Perhaps it was one of those mornings when we were made to listen to the School Radio Service which hissed and crackled from a radio on the wall of the assembly hall. It was a bizarre service as the entire school and staff stood about utterly motionless listening and singing along to a radio. Apparently during prayers, with my head bowed and my eyes closed, I was accused of rocking back and forth. Those around me thought it would be a laugh by joining in and creating a sea of swaying pupils. This did not escape the ever alert Mr Buller who stopped everyone chanting in the middle of the Lord's Prayer demanding to know what was going on. The vicar on the radio defied Mr Buller and carried on regardless. Although I was completely unaware of my actions I was instantly accused by a teacher nearby as the instigator and sent upstairs to the headmaster's office to await my fate. I did not have to wait long for within minutes the office door was flung open and in stormed a raging, red-faced Mr Buller bellowing loudly, 'What were you playing at Carter?'

'Nothing Sir' I replied, still unsure of my alleged crime.

'Nothing!' he ranted, 'Nothing! Mrs Cannerly (I never liked her much anyway) said she saw you rocking and swaying'.

'It wasn't me, Sir' I pleaded, this probably being the last time that I ever uttered those time-honoured words in my defence.

'Don't lie to me boy' he thundered. 'Hold out your hand.'

Thwack, down came the cane sending an electric stinging sensation through my fingers.

'Now get back to your class before I knock your head off.'

Mr Buller was always threatening to knock pupils' heads off. I wonder if perhaps at teacher training college he had been singled out and secretly instructed in the art of decapitation and just yearned for an excuse to use this otherwise totally useless skill. According to at least one of my sons I am still to this day in the habit of rocking to and fro on occasions. Maybe there is a distant relative with a maritime connection who swayed backwards and forwards to the pitch and roll of some great schooner under full sail as it ploughed through the heaving waves. On the other hand there is always the possibility that I was on the brink of falling asleep during prayers. I fancy this is a more likely explanation despite it lacking the romanticism of my former theory.

Apart from Mr Buller putting the fear of God into all of us for much of the time, he did nevertheless have a caring side to him as amply displayed during one annual swimming gala. Janet Wilson was powering her way through the water when the straps on her costume snapped and her top fell down. We all enjoyed this moment immensely. It would have been better if she had been doing the back-stroke, but as she made her way to the side of the pool Mr Buller was first on the scene to rescue her from her embarrassing dilemma by encouraging her through a menacing grin to get out of the water. Not surprisingly, Janet Wilson refused to expose her ample bosom to Mr Buller, or in fact to anyone else which caused Mr Buller to become slightly irritated that anyone should question let alone refuse to comply to his authority. For a moment time stood still as the poolside stand off held everybody's attention. Eventually, poor Janet Wilson was delivered from her plight by a female member of staff coming forward with a towel to wrap around her before escorting her back to the changing rooms. Meanwhile, Mr Buller had adopted his usual rigid stance on the edge of the pool with straight arms and clenched fists glaring around at everyone, anyone of whom could quite easily become the next victim of his wrath, and for no other reason than just being there and breathing! Over the years Mr Buller became an iconic figure in my class insomuch as his mannerisms, his phrases and his tone of voice was mimicked by most of us and even by my father who had never even met the man. I would like to think that as we progressed through the school up to the point when there was barely a handful of us left because we did not want to leave, that a mutual respect evolved between us and Mr Buller, our never to be forgotten idiosyncratic headmaster.

The first two years at the art school were spent segregated from the girls. Obviously we passed them in the corridors and fraternised with them in the school yard, but otherwise there was no contact of any sort. Many pupils left at 16 to go to college or find work and the remaining pupils were lumped together to form one class. This was a strange experience sharing the class with girls as well as a common room which we had now been given for our exclusive use. There was also a canteen room as we called it where we could make tea, have lunch and sell a few sweets to pupils. Some girls had once been caught boiling a few eggs in a saucepan and then in all innocence had used the same water to make some cups of tea. This led to an episode of Mr Buller ranting in assembly one morning about the dangers of such a practice as according to him the water could contain something poisonous from the eggshells which he inferred would, within minutes of drinking the tea, result in the canteen floor being littered with dead and dying schoolgirls. This would reflect badly on the school, he went on, as well as being what I thought would be a number of inconvenient obstacles to step over on my way to the counter to buy a chocolate covered Wagon Wheel. Speaking of which, apart from the fact they are no longer as big as they used to be as is the case with so many things in life, you would not really think that such a thing could bring about a situation. But it can, and I was eating it. The bell had just rung for the start of lessons when I decided to ram the entire Wagon Wheel into my mouth to stave off my hunger. I was hurrying along the corridor, cheeks bulging like an avaricious hamster when Mr Buller stepped out in front of me, a formidable obstacle to find blocking my progress.

'You're late Carter,' he bellowed at me, 'What lesson are you going to?' he demanded, staring through me with penetrating eyes. Finding it difficult to reply as you can probably appreciate I blurted out along with a few slobbery crumbs of Wagon Wheel something like, 'Blime glowin tlu plistery, Slhur'.

'What have you got in your mouth boy?' he continued to bellow.

'Au pflogun plheel, Slhur' I attempted to reply.

'What?' he glared.

'Au pflogun plheel, Slhur' I spluttered.

'You stupid boy' he boomed, 'If I catch you again, I'll knock your head off'.

'Yefs Slhur' I replied, wiping dribbling chocolate from my chin with the back of my hand and went to join my history class.

There were some individual characters among the staff that will long be remembered by many who attended the art school. The geography teacher 'Spider' was so named because he had a gangly figure and seemed to possess arms and legs that were inordinately long as though they were on loan from someone much taller than him. The English teacher always referred to as 'Hawkeye' on account that she never missed a trick was a teacher to be wary of and many a time I wished I had been invisible behind my desk. She always struck me as being of a matronly disposition invariably wearing a cardigan that was fastened at the top by a single button. I wish on reflection I had taken more notice of her during lessons then perhaps my love of literature, in particular that of Victorian writers might have entered my life a little earlier. She once put out a request that as budding artists we should each paint a picture illustrating a favourite poem which we could then enliven the walls of the classroom with. As I recall, no one actually fulfilled this task. Now not wishing to sound like a 'goody-two-shoes', but I always liked the emotive poem *Adlestrop* by Edward Thomas and I can now announce with a degree of smugness that I did complete the exercise albeit over 20 years later by which time the art school had been demolished, so I hung it on my own wall.

I also remember all of us being told to write an essay on our favourite animal. I decided in the hope of getting good marks to impress 'Hawkeye' by writing about an animal I felt sure she would never of heard of, thus lessening any criticism she might have of my literary effort. Banking on the fact that she was unlikely to possess an 1878 edition of *The Popular Natural History* by Revd J.G. Wood, I copied pretty much word for word a description of the Myrmecobius. The Myrmecobius of course as everybody knows, well some people perhaps who have been lucky enough to spot one in the vicinity of the

Swan River in Australia will agree that it gives the impression of having the head of a rat, the body of a cat and the tail of a squirrel and therefore the ideal choice for anyone who wants three pets in one. Feeding it could be a confusing issue as it might require acorns and hazelnuts to nourish the bottom end, a tin of cat food for the middle and the rotting contents of your dustbin for the top end. The truth is I had never heard of a Myrmecobius until I saw a picture of it on page 120 of the book whereupon I hatched my crafty plan. Sadly I cannot remember what sort of mark I got for my essay, but at least there was not a 'See me' in red ink at the bottom of the page so I must have got away with it.

It appears that I was also in for another round of French lessons under the auspices of Miss Sweeting who very much reminded me of the actress Margaret Rutherford, which she may not thank me for the comparison, but Margaret Rutherford was immensely endearing and entertaining. I regret not having paid sufficient attention during her lessons for I never mastered the language and failed to appreciate its importance until I started to travel. I remembered the names of many things but stringing a sentence together in French is another matter altogether and the French become quickly intolerant (let's not forget Agincourt) of you waving and throwing your arms about pointing at things and burbling away in schoolboy French. I normally got by but I could have done much better. Fortunately I have travelled more time in Australia than anywhere else so I only had to learn 'strine' in order to communicate. For the uninitiated 'strine' basically involves speaking English through clenched teeth, developed so the tale goes, to prevent the ever present flies that wait for you, pursue you and drive you to the brink of insanity from getting into your mouth as you talk.

There was a short-lived affair with a young trainee maths teacher who was not really very good at keeping the class in order. He was, apparently, a member of the Territorial Army and during a weekend exercise had jumped out of a plane, presumably with a parachute and broken his leg. On reflection maybe he forgot the parachute. It would seem a somewhat painful length to go to just to get out of teaching us maths, but perhaps he thought it was a justified course of action. Another teacher who occasionally taught us engineering drawing, was one of those individuals, who hover on being a near genius at their chosen subject, yet find anything else in life difficult to grasp and consequently appear to be absent-minded and very vulnerable. We gave him a hard time during lessons. The lessons involved selecting a piece of heavy casting from an engine or some unknown mechanical device which were stored in a cupboard in the classroom. We would then be taught and expected to reproduce a drawing showing the chunk of scrap iron in three differing projections. As restlessness settled in somebody would be chosen as the victim of the lesson and subjected to the following. A long T-square would be placed across the gap between the desk top and the back of the chair in front where the unsuspecting culprit would be beavering away at his drawing. Very quietly as many pieces of cast iron as possible would be balanced along the length of the T-square until it was bending alarmingly under the weight. At this point the instigator at his desk would tap the shoulder of the unsuspecting boy in front who swinging around dislodged the entire load sending it crashing to the floor with a terrifying noise creating pandemonium, followed by raucous laughing from everyone in the class. It was a lark that never failed to cause great hilarity and great disruption. To pile on the agony for the teacher we would sometimes wait for him at going home time to watch him struggle to get his bicycle upright after he had pulled it away from the post it was leaning against and it had crashed to the ground. This was a fairly guaranteed event, because we had filled the saddle bag with house bricks and the weight would take him by surprise.

I put being a mathematical failure down to the fact that the constant noises outside the school of a busy town going about its business were too interruptive for my concentration. Unfortunately, Miss Warren our last maths teacher was not of the same opinion and put it down to a constant lack of effort and not paying attention. However, I did pay attention one afternoon when a fire engine with its sirens screaming roared past the classroom window whereupon I leapt to my feet followed by some other lads to watch it go past. Miss Warren told us all to sit down. 'You've all seen a fire engine before' she shouted, but quick as a flash I retorted, 'Yes Miss, but this one's on fire!' She joined the rest of the class in laughter after admitting it had been a good quip. From my point of view it had been a good lesson and as usual I had, once again, learnt very little. Miss Warren banned me from even attempting to take my 'O' level examination, saying anything I wrote on the paper apart from my name at the top would be a waste of paper and everyone's time. She was obviously a woman with foresight.

Then there was the biology mistress. The previous biology teacher left, although I am sure it was nothing to do with me putting flakes of silver nitrate in the fish tank during a lunch break and reducing the population slightly. I would hate to think she had taken the blame for their mysterious deaths, spending the rest of her life riddled with guilt. Her replacement, however, was something else altogether. She arrived one day, young, friendly, shapely, smiling and tempting and most of the lads in my class fell instantly in love with her as she was, during her lesson, guaranteed to raise the levels of raging testosterone in all of us. Her name was Barbara Pitton and she often conducted the lesson sitting on her desk top in front of the class wearing a short skirt that exposed an admirable and seductive length of thigh at which we were more than happy to ogle. Suddenly learning about plant structures and the reproductive system of the earthworm became peripheral as our interests lay in learning more about Barbara Pitton's structure and reproductive system. A scheme was devised between a few of us whereby one person would call her over to their desk on the pretext of not being able to understand something in the text book. While she leant over that pupil could steal a glance down her partly unbuttoned blouse which was the cue for the lad behind him to drop a pencil on the floor in order to bend down to pick it up and steal a glance up her skirt. It was a system that worked extremely well as we all became clumsier by the minute dropping pencils everywhere. After all we were potential artists and felt it more than necessary to further our art education and knowledge of the human form, or were we just a group of sexually frustrated lads who lusted after Barbara Pitton our minds awash with lascivious thoughts? In the privacy of our own common room we would discuss her, dissect her and revel in fantasies about her, all along the lines of, if only. Predictably, if only, was of course all we had to hang on to.

Biology lessons tend to follow a basic pattern by dabbling in a bit of botany and learning about the sex life of earthworms and frogs and not what we all wanted to know which was about the life cycle of humans. We did watch a film one afternoon that clanked its way through a projector dealing with this guarded subject, but for the main part we were really left to draw our own conclusions. I recall that when I was in my early teens a few years prior to seeing that non-illuminating film, my father had possibly spotted a restlessness about me. It is also possible that he had spotted me gazing out of my bedroom window lusting after a grammar school girl who regularly passed my house wearing a skimpy games skirt and clutching a hockey stick with a determined grip that would have made the eyes of a grown man water. Whatever it was it prompted him into deciding that the time was right to present me with a book entitled *How Life is Handed On* which was supposed to explain everything I needed to know should I find myself in a situation like the encounter with Vanessa Bass on the canal bank, preferably without the grubby knickers. The book monotonously explained the sex life of the earthworm and then the frog as if they held no objection to the fact that a blow by blow account of their sexual exploits seems to be exposed across the pages of every biology text book ever printed. Then it got to humans and wandered off at a tangent. It seemed to be going quite well until some firemen entered the equation with their hosepipes. The analogy was that the tapered nozzle of one fireman's hose should fit snuggly into the receiving end of another fireman's hose so when firmly rammed together no spillage is experienced and that was pretty much that. I stared at the diagram of two hosepipes being coupled together then I stared at the ceiling, then back to the diagram. If you are still following this then I feel sure that you will sympathise with me, for given my young age, it looked to me as if in order to have sex I would have to become a fireman. Luckily for me only three doors down the street lived Mr Logan who was in fact a fireman, and furthermore he had two daughters which proved beyond doubt that he had coupled his hosepipe on at least two occasions. But, hang on a minute, what about all the other kids in the street? Had their dads all belonged at some time to the fire brigade, or could one just join temporarily whenever one wanted sex? It became very confusing and sometimes I simply yearned to be an earthworm. I knew how they did it!

Anyway, being a bit of a self-made naturalist I got on quite well with Barbara Pitton and would often bring her a specimen to look at from my bedroom museum and she would reciprocate with something that she thought might interest me, but not from her bedroom. One day she presented me with a box containing the complete skeleton of a frog that had been immaculately cleaned and bleached but was in reality an absolute nightmare of tiny pieces. Would I like to have a go at reconstructing it for her, she smiled in a way that made me say yes without hesitation, despite having no idea of how I could achieve this. Shortly afterwards she became my guardian angel and my saviour, because she brought in a rabbit skeleton which she thought I might like to put back together for her and I could use the school cellar and do it on a Wednesday afternoon instead of going to games, which of course I detested. I was now inundated with Barbara Pitton's old bones and it could not get better than this. I laboured on my own in the cellar week after week except on the occasions when Barbara Pitton came to see how I was doing and stay for a chat or sort out some of the bones with me. My mates were pretty envious of me because I had got the biology mistress to myself in the school cellar and they wanted to know everything that had happened, what might have happened and what they thought should have happened between us. After all I was heading towards becoming 18 and had long since lost interest in the sex lives of earthworms. After a couple of months of cellar activity, in the minds of my classmates I was having a torrid affair among the old bones with the biology mistress who would be making sure that I never played football or cricket ever again. Well, it sounded promising enough to me, but alas it was never to be. Along with two or three of my mates I even got to show Barbara Pitton some of the Derbyshire dales on a couple of Saturdays when we would meet her at the railway station and ramble around the Peak District for the day. However, despite all the fraternising and shared interests I have to confess that at the final hurdle I failed her. I feel remorse and guilt for never finishing the frog skeleton, for never finishing the rabbit skeleton and worst of all for failing my O level Biology. I have no excuses for the first two inadequacies but I blame the latter on classroom distraction in the shape of a beguiling biology mistress. I had to re-take the exam at night school. I often wonder whether Barbara Pitton ever realised just what a distraction she had been, albeit it a very pleasant one. And yes I do sometimes wonder where you are now Barbara Pitton?

Due to the building being generally unsuitable for use as a school we were subjected to its inadequacies on an almost daily basis. For example, if I wanted to have school dinners which I occasionally did when I tired of my years of packed lunches containing endless rounds of beef dripping sandwiches which is all I ever requested, thus having consumed enough over the years to have arteries as rigid and as blocked as any grossly neglected plumbing system, I was forced to walk up the hill to the canteen at the technical college. I quickly learnt that if I got there towards the end of the dinner break then there would often be seconds of pudding going free and they did a fine college pudding and custard.

For physical education we all had to troop down the road to a dingy hall and suffer the tedium of volleyball each week. All we ever played was volleyball which was so utterly boring that quite often even the teacher could not be bothered to turn up, thus leaving us to our own devices which some of us interpreted as an excuse to go home early. Sometimes you might be exposed to the wrath of Mr Buller the following morning if he happened to find out, but that was just the lottery of life. I suspect the PE teacher took one look at us, decided there and then that there were never going to be any Olympic volleyball players among us so dismissed us as a waste of his time. I never liked him anyway as he was lean, gristly with a weasel-like face the texture of a crumpled brown paper bag. The games periods were held at the Darley playing fields over a mile away to which we had to walk, which was fortunate for me as it was halfway home, but not so convenient if you needed to catch a bus or a train home as a few pupils did. One year the school sports day was held in a park on the south side of the town which to me was unknown territory and so far away as to probably require a passport. This would have been a lot of trouble to go to just so I could throw a javelin badly, this being the only activity I had failed to get out of. Surprisingly I did not win a prize that day as there did not appear to be a specific category for being completely useless at throwing the javelin.

Two further lessons were held up the hill at the College of Art. These were metalwork and woodwork. Metalwork was an entirely new thing to me, so sawing and filing sheets of copper, brazing joints and bashing out patterns with a hammer and punch were all newly acquired skills that enabled me to proudly take home my wondrous creations. Whether my mother actually wanted an undersized copper vase that continually fell over, a copper mug you would not wish to drink from without inviting gastroenteritis, and a copper ash tray for a non-smoker is something she was never asked. They simply arrived. I found woodwork rather more interesting and it did not take me too long to master my first tenon joint, mortise joint and glue two fingers to a piece of wood with scotch glue. I never attained the heady heights of producing a secret-mitred dovetail, but to be perfectly honest it was so complex that as far as I was concerned it was best kept a secret. Restraining myself from immediately forging ahead and constructing a replica Chippendale chair I confined myself to producing a pipe rack. This my mother used as a scissor rack as she refused point blank to take up pipe smoking just so I could revel in the belief that I had actually produced something useful. I think I was beginning to develop a complex about my handicraft accomplishments. I did not want to turn into that strange person quoted by the writer Anthony Hope, who was apparently 'very fond of making things which he doesn't want, and then giving them away to people who have no use for them'. So I set about making a wooden box with a sliding lid for myself to house a model boat I had made at home which unfortunately sank on its maiden voyage with the tragic loss of all hands, an electric motor and two U2 batteries. Undaunted I set about carving a trophy figure for a local sea-scout group, happily chiselling away at a block of wood for several weeks. Okay, so it was no Michelangelo's *David* but it was shaping up nicely, until that is, somebody stole it one weekend and used it for target practice with an air gun, then abandoned it in the college wood store. It did not deserve such an ignominious fate and was looking more than a little worse for wear having been on the receiving end of a shoot-out, but it was very good and kind of whoever stole it to return it so I could now boast of being the proud owner of a completely useless piece of splintered wood. This would definitely be a bonus towards my O level woodwork. I think by now I deserved a lucky break and it came as a 'pièce de résistance' in the form of a mahogany jewel box with carved sides and a carved lid which has not only survived the test of time, but impressed Mr Buller to the extent that he photographed me holding my box so it could be placed in the school album of pupils' memorable achievements. This had to be my one great success story.

The actual art lessons themselves became better as I moved up through the school for all those 'still life' exercises of drawing scattered fruit, a school chair, more scattered fruit, a dust bin and even more scattered fruit lacked both excitement and inspiration and it was not until I could create paintings out of my head that things livened up. I went through a period of surrealism influenced by the works of Dali and would create pictures of perhaps a desert scene with a skeletal rib cage stuck in the sand with taught dried fragments of skin held between the ribs, playing cards propped against the bones and an eyeball looking on. In other words the sort of everyday things I might see from the top deck of the bus taking me to school if by some quirk of fate my breakfast bowl of Weetabix had been mysteriously laced with hallucinogenic mushrooms. On reflection this is a pretty wild bit of speculation as we never had mushrooms of any sort at home as my mother always said that she did not mind them, but they did not like her. You can come to your own conclusion as to just what she was talking about. The art teacher Mr Finton was a likeable teacher and sufficiently understanding not to have me committed knowing I would eventually grow out of it, which I did.

After I had left school and started work, I took my A level art examination at night school and this was the first time I had been confronted by a nude female figure to draw. She was somewhat matronly and a far cry from scattered fruit, although she did seem to have a quantity of scattered flesh which caused me a few problems. My actual A level piece was a drawing of a Kangaroo vine and I recall Mr Finton who was also the tutor for the night school class saying I should draw the whole plant out roughly before working on the detail. I preferred to draw a leaf at a time and work my way down the plant so I ignored his advice. At this stage neither of us could have guessed that my future would eventually lead to me making my mark in the exacting world of botanical illustration, so I hope Mr Finton that you will forgive the expression of smugness on my face as I write this sentence. In fact, as far as my future was concerned and life after the art school, even I could not have imagined it possible to turn out the way it did, but that as they say, is another story.

9

LOVE, LIFE AND A BICYCLE

Probably the most notable change in my personal development at school and in particular in later school life was the finding of friendship, camaraderie and sharing social experiences with my peers that came with an entirely new environment. There was an interchange of ideas and a sharing of interests like music, camping and other outdoor activities. Group consultation took place with matters that concerned us at school including ringing the changes of the infamous Christmas school dance. This was not, I hasten to add the highlight of the school year, but it was fairly mandatory, so having a headache, or two left feet did not wash as an excuse for not attending. As we approached our supposed final year and formed the higher echelons of the school a group of us decided that the annual yuletide gallop around the school hall to the strains of the *Dashing White Sergeant* was wearing a little thin, so we all agreed to break the mould by putting on a comedy sketch. I wrote the basic bare bones for the sketch and everyone involved chipped in with ideas and comments to pad it out. It centred on the unveiling of a statue which in turn required a silly opening speech and some Pythonesque antics (yes, we were ahead of our time) thrown in for good measure. I played the part of the statue and was carried onto the stage horizontally in a convincingly rigid manner before being propped upright on a plinth. I even got a line to say before walking away at the end. We all received a round of applause at the finish for our efforts with our 'one night only' production.

Until this time my school friends had all lived closely around me on the estate which for the most part is where we spent our time or at least within the immediate location. Now I was schooling five days a week in a bustling town and as new friendships evolved it became necessary for me to travel some distance in my spare time to see my mates. The first significant change was to catch a bus on my own to get from home to school each day. There would be no more dawdling and larking about with pals on the way to school because I now had to be up and away for I could not afford to miss the bus. Some mornings it seemed like the bus queue was longer than that at the January sales outside Harrods, in which case I might have to wait for a second or even a third bus before I could get on board. Either way I normally managed a seat on the top deck where I could marinate myself in the lingering fumes and the stale smell of cigarette ends and ash left over from the workers of an hour or so earlier. Being late meant charging through the streets like a mad-man chased by slavering dogs and hoping to arrive in time for registration. My most feared misery was to crash through the side door of the school, rush into an empty corridor, gasping for breath and dripping with sweat only to hear the sound of hymn singing that meant assembly was already under way and I was not among it. My predicament was unenviable as I stood alone nervously fingering my school satchel listening to the assembled mass toiling through 'For those in peril on the sea' and wondering in despair about those, or in this instance me, in peril for being horribly late. Such an episode normally ended with a severe reprimand bordering slightly on a death threat from Mr Buller who apparently seemed very intolerant of the vagaries of public transport and even more so of pupils who in his opinion should get themselves out of bed earlier.

Riding the top deck of a bus especially if I was able to get a front seat was often an exciting experience. The bus would lurch from side to side in an unnerving manner as overhanging tree branches bashed against the window causing me to instinctively flinch and duck. And how when the top deck was full and the bottom deck all but empty did the bus, which must surely have been top-heavy, manage not to topple over when a maverick driver flung it so close to buildings and lamp posts? It occurred to me more than once that I might be impaled on a flailing branch as it speared the bus window, leaving me to arrive at school very late, a branch sticking out of my chest, gruesomely maimed and bleeding copious amounts of blood over the floor of Mr Buller's office while he persisted in bellowing at me about getting out of bed earlier; and would I fetch a bucket and mop to clean up the mess on his floor unless I wanted my head knocked off. Riding the top deck did, in a roundabout way help me to become confident for apart from catching glimpses of Fredericks Ice Cream Factory and a view over the walls of the riding stables of the race course, I also spotted and became a life-long fan of the Land Rovers displayed on Kennings forecourt. One day I plucked up the courage and boldly walked into the reception and asked the price of a Land Rover which for me at the age of 15 was quite unexpected. The salesman gave me a leaflet (which I still have) and wrote on it £650 for the basic model. Despite maths being my worst subject I reckoned at five shillings a week pocket money, provided I never spent a penny on anything else would take me 50 years to save the money. In truth I have just had to work this out on a calculator and then I had to have it checked by someone else. In 50 years there would possibly be the added expense of having a wheelchair ramp or a hoist fitted for a walking frame. This was becoming more expensive by the minute and also quite depressing. I needed to seriously re-think my strategy. I also desperately needed my own transport. My new social life demanded it.

This problem was solved by my school pal Dennis who fancied himself as a bit of an entrepreneur by selling dodgy second-hand bicycles. The use of the words 'second-hand' is probably a tad benevolent of me as I reckon he collected the miscellany of parts from scrap heaps, hedge bottoms and a bit of canal dredging thrown in for good measure. Surprisingly they generally worked, although not necessarily all that well, all that often, or even all parts at the same time, but for the princely sum of £2 10s I became a cyclist. I now cycled to school via the notorious meadows passing couples even at that time of day experiencing nature in the corner of fields. I was also able to get out in the evenings to spend time with my mates on the other side of town. The other thing is that overnight I had unwittingly entered the complex world of mechanics and had to spend my pocket money on such technicalities as brake blocks, inner tubes, handle bar tape and paint. Feeling mechanically confident I fitted a whirring, cutting-edge, rear wheel dynamo that powered the lights until, for example, I was required to stop at traffic lights when everything went black. On such occasions at night you are particularly vulnerable leaving yourself wide open to being compacted into the tarmac by a passing bus and becoming quite literally man and machine as one. Another down side of fitting a dynamo is that should it become too tight a fit against the wall of the tyre then it will cunningly wear away the rubber until the tyre splits open allowing part of the inner tube to bulge through like an escaping intestine. Several tyres later I ditched the dynamo and went back to battery powered lights.

I am convinced that bicycle lamps were purposely made with bad connections which were guaranteed to fail at the most inconvenient of times, and there was just such a time when I was stopped by a police car and informed that my rear light was not functioning. Normally such a mundane event would not be worth a mention except that on this particular occasion, strange though it may seem, and it will seem strange for I was wearing a lifebelt. It was very heavy, very cumbersome and not to be recommended as a piece of cycling attire. I had discovered it suspended high in the branches of a tree by the river Derwent, an aftermath of a recent severe flooding. I had, fortuitously, wrapped some newspaper around it to cover up the letters emblazoned around the sides stating that it was the property of the local council. The policeman eyed it with suspicion, tapped it a couple of times and asked me what it was. Unable on the spur of the moment to think of anything clever I admitted that it was in fact a lifebelt. His bemused expression seemed to imply that I was the first cyclist he had ever come across wearing a lifebelt and did I perhaps know something he did not. Maybe for one brief moment he had mistakenly taken me to be a latter-day Noah having prior knowledge of some impending watery catastrophe, especially as I was cycling uphill to higher ground and the sanctuary of Nottingham Road Cemetery. I thumped my rear light and thankfully it burst into life. The police man gave the lifebelt a final tap, stood back and thoughtfully stroked his chin then got back into his car and much to my relief drove away. If only he had known how close he was to bagging his first theft of a lifebelt by an under-lit cyclist!

I painted my bicycle frame bright yellow and applied yellow handle bar tape. Interestingly enough, yellow according to the psychology of colours is associated with insanity which possibly helped each time I ventured out on the thing. I recall the first time I cycled across the town to visit my grandmother. Granny lived on the other side of the town to me and quite near to the old cemetery on Uttoxeter New Road. As a kid visiting her on a dark winter's night walking with my parents the inadequately lit road alongside the graveyard was a very spooky experience. I imagined all manner of scary things lurking in the shadows among the tombstones as we went to catch a sparking, whirring trolley bus back into town. Anyway, she took one dismayed look at my bicycle saying that it in her opinion, and I have no idea when she was last on a bicycle if indeed she ever rode one, that it was the most appalling and hideously unsafe contraption on two wheels she had ever clapped eyes on. In short she condemned it as a death trap and I would in all probability be dead before the weekend. These were harsh words indeed and I felt a little deflated by her reaction to my machine. Mind you, the idea of being dead before the weekend did not go down too well either. However, every cloud has a silver lining and dear old granny became so concerned that she paid for a brand new bicycle of my choice so I could ride in both style and safety. I bought a shiny blue Falcon and an Ernie Clements shoulder bag, and was I the business with my new machine in the school yard the following Monday morning? In those days it was almost comparable to arriving to school in a Porche without of course, the same girl-pulling power as I cannot recall being suddenly surrounded by a crowd of sexy school girls sidling up to me and begging with pouting lips to straddle my cross-bar. I am certain I would have remembered that.

Anyway, even Dennis did not seem to be miffed that he was now a customer down and had no chance of selling me another and better second-hand model (for better read less rust). I base this on the fact that such was our friendship he invited me on holiday with his parents that summer for a week in Christchurch where the highlight of the stay was when his father almost drove the car over the top of a harbour wall somewhere and Dennis's mother in the front seat got extremely stressed out shouting we could all have been drowned and generally worked herself up into a bit of a state. It all went very quiet in the car for a long time after that. The main thing is that the bicycle was a real saviour and enabled me to extend my social life to such far-flung places as Ripley where my good mate Pete lived. I often rode back in the dead of night and cannot actually remember much about Ripley, except I am sure that at some stage of her singing career Susan Maughan did a stint there one night where she constantly insisted on how desperate she was to become *Bobby's Girl.* I do not think Bobby had much to say on the matter and he was in all likelihood not in Ripley on the night anyway. Now I come to think of it there was a kind of family connection with Ripley for decades ago my grandfather used to have a market stall there and sold gramophone records and condoms, an incongruous combination by anyone's standards. On second thoughts you could in fact use both at the same time. When my father was young and innocent he used to help his father out on the stall on a Saturday, but a lot of the customers ignored him as they were too embarrassed to ask him for a packet of condoms and he was too young to know what they were for.

Because I now cycled everywhere it opened up a new world to me and over the coming years I must have covered hundreds of miles and even on one occasion pedalled myself into a state of total exhaustion. I decided to do a round trip of about 130 miles from south of Derby to north of Manchester. I left at seven in the morning and pedalled my way to Buxton via Ashbourne. I felt that the hard slog up Long Hill out of Buxton shortened my life by a couple of years, but after that it was fairly easy going through Manchester city centre and out past Strangeways prison. By early evening I had begun the return trip and already felt quite weary by the time I came to tackle the uphill climb out of Whaley Bridge to Buxton in the lowest of gears. I was moving at barely walking pace. I finally gasped my way to the top, my head about to burst open, my heart not far behind and both legs feeling like molten lead. But worst of all was the now almost unbearable fiery burning of my crotch. Bicycle seats seem to be made so thin, so hard and so uncomfortable that the last thing you really want to do is actually sit on one for more than five minutes at a time. I had been on mine for hours and I was suffering. My tired legs begged me to sit down while my throbbing groin begged me to stand up. It was time for the last resort, which was not an easy decision. For such a situation as I now faced I had read somewhere that a certain amount of relief could be found by the application of a ladies sanitary towel. You can see now why this is a last resort. Having free-wheeled downhill into Buxton I sought out a shadowy backstreet where undetected I slipped a sanitary towel inside my underpants. Yes I was carrying one with me in anticipation of this happening. You do not think I was going to march into a chemist shop and ask for one did you? That old saying about never leave the house without wearing clean underpants in case you have an accident sprung to mind, for just how embarrassing would it be for me to now to find myself the victim of an accident and be discovered in hospital wearing a sanitary towel. Hopefully, I would be found unconscious and remain that way. I ploughed on into the night a sweat sodden mass of burning muscle silently screaming in pain until somewhere down the road I slumped over my handlebars, fell off my bike and died in the hedge bottom of someone's front garden. It was way past midnight and no traffic passed by and nobody came out of the house to inspect the steaming bundle of body and bike beneath their hedge. My legs had turned to jelly and my groin even with the aid of the pad was on fire and there seemed to be little doubt that my genitals had either worn away or had fallen off hours ago, but somehow I was past caring. It was peaceful beneath the hedge and it was only the prospect of falling asleep and being woken in the morning by some dog passing by and cocking his leg over me that spurred me to get up and finish the ride which I did at around three o'clock that morning. The soreness lingered for several days and I was convinced that had I been a woman then I had just ruined any chance of bearing children in the future.

Girls of course was what most of us wanted at the time, or at least we thought we wanted them and at school we were surrounded by them on a daily basis, and yet things were never as simple as they looked, at least not for me. For example, I had a girlfriend from school for a few weeks but it quickly died a death. Then egged on by my mates I clumsily accosted a girl I fancied in the school yard one day called Jaqueline Rowse who turned me down on the spot. As you can imagine this did nothing for my already frail confidence when it came to liaisons with the opposite sex, so I decided that perhaps I was really a lad's lad which seemed a lot easier to cope with. However, it was impossible not to be aware of the enticing young girls that grouped themselves about the school yard at break times. Ever inventive and not wishing to miss a golden opportunity a band of us found some satisfaction as well as a source of entertainment, courtesy of me being able to use the cellar whenever I wished.

As with all cellars there had to be an access chute and this one was no exception. The large grate over the top was part of the yard above and consequently pupils stood over it as a matter of course. This proved to be to our advantage in the case of girls occupying a stance on the grate allowing us a worm's eye view up their skirts. This became a very popular break time activity in the cellar and I could have sold tickets. If the viewing was not particularly interesting enough then a scout was sent up to engage in conversation with the tastiest girl he could find while at the same time drawing her ever closer to the grate. If she came with friends then that was a bonus. In reality I guess we were a pathetic sight, but for many of us who had yet to sample the delights of the female body this provided us with a fleeting glimpse of erotica on a par with Janet Wilson's bathing costume coming adrift in the swimming gala. Okay, so it was unashamed voyeurism, but it was also a jolly good ruse and since young Sarah the only delectable girl in our small class was already spoken for then we had to seek our pleasures where we could. There was, in truth another girl in my class who fired us up and she was a well-spoken girl called Diana who was a terrible tease and a frustrating flirt, and the image of her sitting on the radiator pipes in the common room baiting us with more than a flash of thigh is something you carry in your mind for a long time. Sex or lack of it was a subject that everyone discussed at some time or other in the common room and often centred on a mate who spent much of his weekend playing football and the rest of the time playing athletic games of carnal lust with his obviously very rampant young girlfriend. And yes we were all envious and it set me thinking whether I should be less concerned with conquering rock climbs and exploring holes in the ground and make more of an effort to conquering and exploring the mysteries of a girl's anatomy. The thing is, they always wanted to be taken out, so how was I ever going to be able to save enough money to buy my first Land Rover and finance a romance at the same time? Why was my young life so full of contradiction, complexity and indecisiveness?

All was not lost for during the summer holidays one year a girl came into my life when I took a job in a small private zoo in the Peak District. To get there entailed a long, hilly and exhaustive ride on my trusty steed, therefore I only came home when I had run out of clean clothes which by then would require some very serious washing, as indeed I did myself. My mother trying not to pass out with the smell said that both I and my clothes smelt of a life-threatening cocktail of animal faeces, and we were dealt with in a similar fashion except that I avoided being hung up on the clothes line. Anyway, the young girl who already worked at the zoo called Linsey and I appeared to get on quite well together and spent what little spare time we had down at the village shop or strolling the lanes. The actual lifestyle we led at the zoo was unbelievably bizarre for we shared the house not only with the pleasantly eccentric owners, but also with a curious collection of people that came and went during my time there. Towards the end of the summer holiday a group of us left the zoo including Linsey who we all but kidnapped for she was the only full-time employee among us. Kidnapping her did not please the owners too much. I returned to school and our liaison continued. Linsey lived on the other side of town from me which was not very convenient and got herself a job as a kennel maid at the nearby greyhound track which was housed within the austere walls of the one-time Derby jail that in its past had hung more than its fair share of criminals. Quite regularly I would cycle from home across town to my aunt and uncles, collect their Alsatian dog and walk it to the track and wait for Linsey to finish work, whereupon I would gallantly walk her home. At this stage you will be full of admiration for my selfless show of chivalry and how more romantic could I get than waiting in the darkness beneath the oppressive walls of the former prison for my girlfriend to escort her home? Due to her often late finish, by the time I had seen her home, walked the dog back, mounted my bicycle and ridden all the way home it felt like it was getting on for breakfast time, and all this for a kiss or two!

It was sometime during all this that I acquired one of my best curiosities. Linsey knew that I was a collector of almost anything I considered collectable, so she told me about her grandfather who years ago, while working on a building site in Nottingham, had broken into a small cave in the area of the old hermitage and found a stone casket. Somehow it had ended up in the dusty vaults of Derby museum where it had languished for the past decade, but it was mine if I wanted to collect it. Quick as a flash I was round to the museum to collect my bounty. It was handed over to me but there was no information about what it might have been. It was made from a solid piece of stone, carved on all the sides with a stone lid and a recumbent lion as the handle. It also bore traces of a lead lining. It was blindingly obvious that this casket was in fact a Victorian burial urn, but whether it had been for a human or a pet I will never know for the ashes had long gone. Despite its weight I set off to the bus stop with it under my arm. Once on the bus I balanced it on my lap where I noticed more than a few sideways glances in my direction and oddly enough nobody came to sit next to me. Surely they did not think I had done a bit of grave robbing? When I got it home I proudly showed it to my mother. She had misgivings about. 'You don't know who, or what's been inside it' she commented in an unenthusiastic tone. Perhaps this attitude clouded her judgement when I suggested I could clean it out and we could keep loose tea or biscuits in it. It seemed my suggestions were not welcome. The relationship between Linsey and I was becoming a tad wearisome and I needed to re-think the whole thing especially as exams were looming ever closer. Perhaps she had spotted the gleam in my eyes after I had been to the museum and quickly realised that a burial urn was going to be a very hard act to follow! I felt I could not really handle the demands of a relationship, swot up on the parts of a flower head, remember where Valparaiso was, list the Plantagenets, read *The Moonstone* and find my other sock that I was wearing last night. Predictably the relationship wilted. Linsey, in what I assume was a last minute burst of unbridled passion took the double bus journey from her home to visit me one afternoon only to find me deep in study for forthcoming exams and unnecessarily stroppy, well not for a teenager, and refusing to come downstairs to see her. She eventually left and I never saw her again. I feel duty bound to make an apology here and now and in keeping with this book, I wonder where are you now Linsey?

My next attempt to get myself a girlfriend failed almost before it began. I was attracted to a girl at school called Brenda who had a Polish sounding surname that might prove difficult to pronounce under the influence of drink - not that I was drinking at that age, but I felt it important to look to the future. The fact that she only lived about a mile from me was a plus and from the feedback on the school grapevine things appeared quite promising. There seemed to be a lot of intimated intention between us but no positive action.

She always smiled at me whenever I saw her at school despite not having actually asked her out and in the street when we were going home. I remember gazing longingly at her walking from school one day as I was walking in a different direction to catch my bus. If cupid was hovering somewhere to unite us I think he should at least have given me some warning of the lamp-post that I walked smack into and the short trip into outer space that followed. Feeling more than a little foolish I lacked the courage to glance back and see if my antics had registered.

However, summer holidays were upon me and I had organised a camping trip with some school mates clambering around Snowdonia for a while which halted any immediate development on the girlfriend front. The fearless group ready to take on the challenge of the Welsh mountains gathered one morning at the station to catch the train to Crewe and then on to Llanrwst (and I thought Brenda's surname was difficult to pronounce) with the exception of one member of the party who dipped out at the last minute. The message relayed to us by his mother was her son could not join us because he had a virus. None of us was really too sure just what a virus was, but she refused to say anymore on the matter regarding either the symptoms or the effects. We grew a little suspicious of this last minute feeble sounding excuse. A virus as anyone will tell you now is quite simply 'a large group of minute parasitic entities regarded as either the simplest micro-organisms or as complex molecules, consisting of a protein coat surrounding a core of DNA or RNA, capable of growth and multiplication only in living cells, which cause common diseases in animals and plants'. If only she had said this at the time then everything would have been perfectly clear to us…or would it?

Despite being a member short we continued on and slogged our way over to Snowdon, slogged our way up the killer Pig track with ridiculously overweight backpacks, missed the last train down the mountain and had no alternative but to follow the railway track in complete darkness down the mountainside. Near the bottom we pitched camp and stayed for the rest of the holiday. Pete who had thoughtfully, or thoughtlessly depending on your viewpoint, brought along his transistor radio so he could turn up the volume for the benefit of passing walkers and bemused sheep every time Frank Ifield came on singing *I Remember You* as I am sure all the walkers did along with the sheep. And if they had the misfortune to miss that then they could be lucky enough to catch John Leyton singing about his dead girlfriend wailing in the rain-lashed tree tops *Johnny Remember Me.* There seemed to be a lot of people wanting to be remembered at that time which served to remind me to send a postcard to Brenda asking her to meet me outside Northcliffe House when I returned from my mountain exploits. Now this is where it all went wrong because due to an oversight on my part I failed to turn up and because of that I never actually found out whether or not she had turned up. It is more than probable that neither of us turned up and something that I am never likely to know. I recall a decade or so later on having returned from some overseas jaunt, taking a flat for a year off Burton Road and seeing a strikingly, good looking young woman pass me in the street on several occasions, but there was no hint of recognition. This could be due to the fact that my face was rather hirsute at the time, but over the years I have wondered now and then whether Brenda, for that is who it was, ever recalls that bearded man tinkering with a Land Rover in the street and his equally hairy Alsatian dog lounging in the gateway to the house? I somehow doubt it.

Unstoppable time marched on and although I hung on at the art school along with a mere handful of my mates for as long as I could it really seemed as if it was time to leave. Mr Buller certainly thought it was time for us to leave as he set about finding job interviews for us to attend which we interpreted as more than a subtle hint. He once sent three of us for the same position which one of us succeeded in getting while he chastised me and my pal for failing the interview. I feel sure that Mr Buller was eager to get rid of us because we were now the oldest pupils at the school and he had been forced to make us all prefects and I strongly suspect that he did not really think we were prefect material.

One day in February I handed in my prefect badge and went to work for three years at the School Museum Service at the bottom of Duffield Road. A few days after leaving school I went into town to set up an account at Martin's Bank in the Market Square. I was accompanied by my mother who had to vouch for me just to prove to them that I did in fact belong to somebody and had not simply wandered in because it was pelting with rain outside. Getting my first payslip was a bit of a let-down as it was not, in my opinion the same as getting proper money in a brown envelope. I did have first-hand experience of a proper pay packet when I once had a holiday job working on a bread delivery van for the Co-op bakery providing a service to remote farmsteads and villages in south Derbyshire. It was an early start but the real bonus was that while the van driver spent all his lunchtimes in a pub, I was given free rein to devour as many jam tarts, conference tarts and Battenburg cake as I liked. This suited me fine and with a weekly salary of £6 10s along with stuffing myself stupid with cakes I was well on my way to becoming rich and very fat, well for a few weeks at any rate! After revealing all at the bank I was later given a National Insurance number and also a tax code. It all had a ring of 'GOTCHA' about it and I now felt that I was in the 'SYSTEM' up to my neck and it would, of course, pursue me constantly throughout my entire life like a bloodhound hot on the scent of an escaped convict. I was poised at the beginning of a new chapter of my life and I just had to get on with it. There were no other options.

10

LEFT OVERS AND LOOSE ENDS

Before leaping headlong to disappear in the world of work and responsibility I feel inclined to hang onto my childhood a tad longer and compare a few noticeable changes that have taken place over the last half a century and more. Things that have gone forever and things that are no more. For example, the neighbourliness and camaraderie that existed in a street when I was growing up seems to have all but gone. I remember mothers would gossip for hours on a summer evening over the garden fence, or even initiate with the aid of a wind-up gramophone an impromptu dance on the back lawn. This would be no sophisticated tea dance but more along the lines of the *Hokey-Cokey* and the *Conga*, and being a strictly adult affair I had to make do with sneaking a view from behind the curtains of my sister's bedroom. It was pretty tame and innocent stuff that did not deteriorate into a salacious orgy. The only hint of lust came in the form of the occasional flash of Mrs Stevenson's thigh and a general ogling by the chaps of Mrs Maunder's ample bosom which bounced uncontrollably to the point of being dangerously threatening during her overenthusiastic display of the 'shake it all about' bit of the *Hokey-Cokey*. The consensus of male opinion was that had they broken free from the confines of Mrs Maunder's blouse then there was little doubt they would have blackened the eye of anyone unfortunate enough to find themselves within range.

Having my mother's sister and family living opposite created a ready-made form of sociability as we cousins played together in the street. I imagine that by now most street games will have died a death with perhaps the possible exception of some still being played out in school playgrounds. Today's traffic does not encourage street games. Certain street sounds like children screaming, shouting and chanting skipping rhymes are in all probability never heard anymore. Is it now a virtually lost skill to be able to blow a high-pitched screech with a folded privet leaf. Okay so it was a bit limited in its musicality and was never going to lead to a fulfilling career, although I do recall somebody having a go at just that. I was languishing at the end of a stifling hot day in a shabby hotel in Mt Isa, Queensland, watching a show on television called *Australia's Got Talent* when an old, gnarled aborigine guy came on stage allegedly keeping this ancient skill alive by blowing with the aid of a eucalyptus leaf an excruciating rendition of *Waltzing Matilda* and proving in the process, that on this particular occasion, Australia did not have any talent.

The main thing is that my cousins had a television and we did not. Therefore as a family we were often invited over to watch the *Jimmy Jewel and Ben Warriss Show,* or the immensely entertaining Max Wall. Fortunately all eyes would be on the flickering screen and only my father seemed to notice that my uncle (he of the fishing maggots) was feverishly occupied in scratching an area of flaking dry skin on the side of one leg. My father being a fastidious man took exception to this and visibly cringed on the rare occasions when my uncle paid us a visit as he feared our carpet would be showered with my uncle's highly unwelcome dermic offerings. Consequently, my mother would be forced to get out the Goblin hoover after every visit. His wife, my aunt Edna, seemed to 'huff and puff' her way through life as if everything was an effort. She used to work in accounts at the Co-op in town and during the hot days of summer she would get off the bus and waddle (she was a large pear-shaped woman) down the street sweating profusely and announcing that she felt like a 'floggin' grease spot'. Quite what a 'floggin' grease spot' feels like is anybody's guess, so because of this she was always known in my house, affectionately, of course, as 'Floggin Edna'.

As a child I was constantly being made to visit what at the time seemed like masses of relations, many of whom lived on the other side of town. In those distant times families were not so scattered or transitory as they are today and indeed many people lived, worked and died in the same town in which they had been born. I rarely objected to visiting my paternal grandparents even before my granny bought me a new bicycle. As youngsters my sister and I would sometimes sleep at their small terraced house with its musty cellar and small strip of rear garden. One of the lures was that granny always had a biscuit barrel which we were allowed to dip into and which invariably held a stock of chocolate biscuits. At home we did not tend to have much in the way of chocolate biscuits as my mother went for the plainer sorts like malted milk, custard creams and bourbons which my father insisted on calling 'bare-bums' thus highlighting further this worrying preoccupation of his with rectal ruminations. There were also Sport biscuits which depicted 'pipe cleaner' type figures engaged, not surprisingly in a variety of athletic activities; and no, they did not include 'indoor' athletic activities. This was a strictly family biscuit.

My granny spent many evenings at whist or beetle drives (I always thought the latter had something to do with racing beetles) returning around 10 o'clock with an armful of newspaper brimming with fish and chips which we all shared. The chip shop where she bought them was presumably owned by a Dolly Hunt for it was always referred to as 'Dolhunts' spoken as one word. My granny loved her food and would not give a second thought to polishing off a couple of pig's trotters before retiring for the night. There was something unsettling about watching granny devour what in reality is the foot of a dead pig. To my way of thinking this is akin to eating any other appendage of a pig like its tail and ears, and let me throw in its snout and genitals while I am about it. My point being, who in their right mind would wish to eat such things? Suddenly, I feel unwell.

My grandfather was a very versatile man who could play the piano, relate stories and jokes, perform magic tricks and could, quite literally turn his hand to making anything and everything. He was always fun. When he himself was a small child he brought a helium filled balloon home from a fair which he let go in the living room. Naturally it floated upwards and momentarily hovered around the gas light before a loud explosion blew the entire lamp and fittings out of the ceiling. That was the sort of man my grandfather was! Despite having been a prisoner of war and survived both the Somme and Passchendaele, it had not in any way lessened his sense of humour. On a summer's afternoon he could often be found fast asleep on a sofa having dropped off while watching the test match on his black and white television set. I always remember that very early television as it had a coin-sized metal disc on the front just beneath the screen bearing the head of a man along with the word Baird. The image of course, was that of John Logie Baird, a Scotsman who really got his act together with black and white televisions and later colour. It is said that during his electrical experimentations he unintentionally gave himself a 1,000 volt electric shock and lived to tell the tale. I bet that made his hair stand on end! Anyway, while he was deep in sleep (my grandfather, not Baird, he was already having his ultimate nap) his cat would curl up on his stomach and also fall asleep. Both man and cat lay lost to the world, the cat gently rising and falling in time to my grandfather's breathing as if it was riding out the waves at sea. It only needed an 'Owl' and a 'pea-green boat' to complete the enactment of Edward Lear's famous nonsense poem.

My grandparent's house shared a rear garden with a family who had a daughter Carol who attended one of those 'special' schools. She often ran around the garden making alarming and frightening noises. Well as a small boy I found them alarming and frightening. I once found myself in a very vulnerable situation with Carol. I had stayed overnight at my granny's and had shared the bedroom with my sister. In the morning my sister decided that it would be great fun if I went and stood inside a big wardrobe in the corner of the bedroom. I could not quite grasp what fun could be had by me standing in a wardrobe, but remembering the 'dinner over my head' episode and already learning not to incur the wrath of a woman, or in this instance my sister, I stupidly climbed into the wardrobe. Quicker than it takes to shake a stick at a dog she slammed the door shut and turned the key. Entombed inside the wardrobe wearing only my pyjama top I wondered just how much fun this actually was. My thoughts kept veering on the side of no fun at all. This was not the land of Narnia. In fact this was the land of total darkness coupled with an overwhelming smell of mothballs amidst a claustrophobic collection of granny's large frocks. I banged on the door demanding my release, but my sister had left the room. As you will be very sympathetic to my situation I know you will agree with me when I say that in such fearful circumstances it is quite permissible to wet one's pants. I had been denied this last rite. I was not wearing any! Teetering on the brink of releasing the contents of my bladder over granny's frocks the door unexpectedly flew open to reveal my giggling sister and to my absolute horror pointing at my willy and advancing towards me was an over excited Carol uttering all manner of intimidating noises. In sheer panic I crashed out of the wardrobe and fled beneath the bed where I lay scared out of my wits, half naked and forever haunted by the unforgettable spectacle of the howling, bellowing Carol seemingly hell-bent on grabbing hold of whatever she could of my exposed and not very private, privates. It is precisely this kind of incident that can scar a chap for life and become a serious set-back, never mind the not having been breast fed scenario!

However, life was not all trauma and granny sometimes gave us money to go to a matinee show at the Cosmo cinema just up the road, or money for sweets at a corner shop. This area of Derby, off Uttoxeter New Road, was very much the domain of the corner shop: from grocery shops, sweet shops, wool shops, barbers and off-licenses. The nearest corner shop for me was run by a kindly Mrs Potts and her daughter Ivy who was once rumoured to have had a crush on my father when he was a young man. Unfortunately, poor Ivy never got a look in from the day my father happened to peer over the wall at the end of his garden and spied a young woman sitting in a chair in her garden. It was almost love at first sight, and she became my mother. As for Ivy, well she never married and when the shop was finally pulled down to make way for new houses she left to live out her days in deepest Cornwall. I well remember that corner shop for even my father had bought his sweets from it when he was a mere lad. Whenever I pushed open the door a bell rang above my head and I would become engulfed in a mixed aroma of mustiness, Parma-violets and earthy potatoes which lay in an open hessian sack on the bare wooden floorboards of the shop. It is a smell of the past and has gone forever. It was still possible to buy a farthings' worth of sweets, but I had to find more money if I wanted love hearts, a pouch of sweet tobacco, a packet of sweet cigarettes or a stick of twisted liquorice. I once bought myself a blue coloured ice-lolly because it was new and different. Blue coloured food is not a smart idea. It was supposed to look like a rocket, but it tasted so horrible that it might easily have been made from old rocket fuel and the wringings out from an astronaut's sweaty sock. I threw it into the gutter and bemoaned my waste of pocket money. I wonder if it was the prototype for Blue-Streak?

On the opposite side of the street lived another aunt and uncle (with the Alsation dog) who were my Godparents. Every week they sent by post the *Eagle* comic for me and its companion comic the *Girl* for my sister. In those days these two comics were considered a bit posh and a cut above the others like the *Beano, Dandy* and the *Beezer*. I could also usually rely upon my aunt and uncle to arrive on Bonfire night with an armful of fireworks. My sister and I always made a Guy Fawkes for our bonfire by stuffing some old clothes of my father's with screwed up sheets of newspaper. Almost every back garden had its own bonfire and firework display which we watched from a bedroom window. Apart from the ubiquitous sparklers, there would be rockets fired from an empty milk bottle, showers of Golden Rain, gushing cones of Vesuvius, and Roman Candles firing coloured balls into the air. Surely the Romans did not light a couple of these in the living room of an evening so they could read the sports page and see what was on at the Coliseum that week? We also had the now banned, unpredictable Jumping Jacks that chased me wherever I ran, and it would be more than once I had to flee into the outside lavatory for safety. Finally there was the Catherine Wheel that normally flew off the post it had been pinned on to cause havoc among the spectators. St Catherine no doubt, viewed this as divine justice on the people cheering and whooping at the spinning, sparking wheel which did, after all, symbolize her hideously, agonising martyrdom. You can see her point!

A few doors on lived yet another aunt who for reasons now lost in the mists of time I always called granny aunty. She never married, lived alone, kept cats and knitted for England. She would sit by her fireside with a cat curled up on her lap surrounded by balls of wool. It is nothing short of a miracle that the cat did not get knitted into the sleeve of a cardigan or become part of a woolly hat. She was also stone deaf which made paying her a visit pretty hard work and quite unbearable after I had spent half an hour shouting at her while she smiled back at me benignly not having understood a single word I had said. The thing about her that always puzzled me was when she came to family gatherings or parties and there were balloons involved. If one came near her or she thought somebody was going to burst one then she would always put her hands over her ears and try to draw away. I never understood this for surely the balloon would simply burst silently and disappear before her eyes, so how scary could that be?

My maternal grandparents lived in the adjacent street, which no doubt you have already worked out for yourself. Sadly my grandfather died when I was only a couple of years old so I cannot remember anything about him. According to my mother I have inherited some of his traits as I apparently walk with the same gait as he did and as she was also want to say, 'If I'd been a dog, I wouldn't pass a bone in the street'. Why do I get the impression that this was not a good trait to inherit? What few stories I have of my grandfather strongly suggest that he was a man to be wary of. He implemented an almost Victorian type of discipline on the household to the extent that if anyone was found sitting in his chair by the fireside they would be courting a death sentence. His rule at the table was that only one glass of water was to be made available during a meal and this had to be shared in order of seniority by everyone. They were a family of five and as my mother was the youngest she got the last drink. There would be little left in the glass and what was there contained numerous bits of food from the mouths of the others, thus creating in essence a left over cold, scant, vegetable soup. She often went thirsty. In view of the fact that the water was pumped from a well along with dead worms and beetles that had fallen in by a hand pump near the kitchen sink, I can see how dying of thirst could become a preferable choice. For the remainder of her life she always drank copious amounts of tea, anywhere and at any time of the day which must surely have been the result of a dehydrated childhood.

I have to confess that I was never too enthusiastic when it came to visiting this 'other granny' for she tended to sit for most of the day by the range dressed in a 'pinny' with a mop-cap on her head in semi gloom looking not unlike a Vermeer painting. This room looked out onto a yard hemmed in on three sides by high brick walls which I sometimes whitened for her with lime wash in an attempt to alleviate the sombre aspect while at the same time earn a bit of extra pocket money. Beyond, at the far end of the narrow garden sat the outside lavatory complete with wooden seat, squares of newspaper on a string and a complexity of cobwebs and dead spiders. It was not a place in which to linger especially at night which my mother detested as a child and she would run back up the garden path clutching a candle and scamper upstairs hoping not to crush a cockroach underfoot as she went. My granny hung onto the old ways and religiously 'whitened' her front door step. She rarely, if ever used the front sitting room keeping everything covered in white sheets and the curtains partly drawn. To draw the curtains completely would have meant there had been a death in the house. She often seemed a tad dour and not blessed with outbursts of humour with the possible exception perhaps, of wartime. When the German bombers droned overhead at night and shrapnel was ricocheting off the garden wall my grandfather, who enjoyed a few pints, would stand defiantly in the garden waving a clenched fist in the air and shouting all manner of abuse and unspeakable curses at the passing planes. My grandmother from within the safety of an Anderson shelter would yell at him above the sound of the nearby 'Ack-Ack' guns to 'Get inside you silly fool. If they see your bald head in the moonlight, they'll drop a bomb on it and we'll all be blown to smithereens'. It does leave me wondering what sort of Luftwaffe pilot would mistake the top of my grandfather's bald head for Rolls-Royce engineering works, or the locomotive sheds which were their intended targets. Bombing my grandfather's bald head would not have furthered the cause of the Third Reich or put a smile on Hitler's face. Did Hitler ever smile? Anyway, the fact is he was a Scotsman (my grandfather, not Hitler) and a plumber from Glasgow which makes me a quarter scot and no doubt responsible for my love of the Highlands. I am proud to be able to wear the Shaw Hunting tartan despite one of its early ancestors being a highland warrior known and feared by many. He was called Bucktooth Shaw which sounds like a killer version of Bugs Bunny clad in a kilt!

There were even more relatives living up the road in Buxton. Here I had another aunt and uncle and a great aunt who was the mayoress of Buxton during World War Two. My aunt Sarah and uncle Bert lived in an end terraced cottage with a sunny porch full of geraniums and an outside lavatory. Uncle Bert who drove steam engines was also a bit of a comic and I always remember the tale about why he had a ridge of scars on the back of his neck. When he was a young man he took up the notion that he could enhance his physique with a chest expander. It was one of those devices that consisted of tightly coiled metal springs and during a session of stretching it out behind his head his strength suddenly failed and the chest expander clamped down hard upon the back of his neck trapping several folds of skin. During the ensuing few minutes as he shouted and jumped about in agony with the metal springs flailing wildly in all directions a couple of people fortuitously came to his rescue and managed to pull the thing off. I think he must have taken up another hobby after that incident. He finished his career as an engine driver running the diesel service between Miller's Dale and Buxton after which he retired and became a Justice of the Peace and a dedicated ale drinker. I have misgivings about the compatibility of these two undertakings. As you can now appreciate, visiting all these relatives was a time consuming business and constantly subject to derogatory comments if I called on one but fail to call on another. In hindsight there is a lot to be said for staying at home.

Home, naturally enough had its own disciplines which had to be observed. Meals for example were always around the table, particularly evening meals where it was compulsory for the whole family to be in attendance, as would be the case at weekends when dinner was eaten at lunchtime. If dinner was eaten in the evenings at teatime, it was still called dinner. We only had lunch at lunchtime in the week and tea at teatime at weekends, although some people called dinner at teatime, supper, whereas supper for me was eaten just before retiring to bed and well after dinner or tea depending on what day of the week it was. Is that clear or should I go through it again? Certain rituals regarding food also had to be observed. Having tinned fruit with evaporated milk was a bit of a luxury and considered to be too rich to eat by itself and was always accompanied by a side plate of bread and butter to tone down the taste buds. Tinned salmon was also a luxury and would only be consumed as a tea time treat on a Sunday. Fish was only served on a Friday because this was the only day the fishmonger did the rounds of the streets in his fish van. He would sound his horn and knock on peoples' doors in the hope of making a few sales. He might on occasion, absentmindedly leave the van door ajar. This was the cue for a neighbourhood cat to seize the moment by leaping into the van and carrying off a piece of cod. This normally happened while the fishmonger was being distracted by the plunging décolletage of Mrs Maunder's flimsy summer dress as he tried desperately to concentrate on whatever it was she was ordering. Mrs Maunder had a way of distracting delivery men by simply drawing breath, so voluminous was her frontage. Either way the cat was happy, the fishmonger was enthralled, albeit a cod short and Mrs Maunder was no doubt more than satisfied with the fishmonger's fishy offerings, as indeed she would be with the baker's crusty cob, the milkman's gold top, the coalman's nutty slack and the rentman, well, the most she could expect from him would be a deferred payment. There were many types of deliveries in those days of all types of goods and it was an essential and social part of life in the suburbs. Nowadays we all troop off like automatons to a local supermarket to experience the dubious pleasure of pushing a trolley with a rogue wheel around the aisles to fill it with things we never really intended to buy.

Birthdays, Easter and in particular Christmas were always celebrated by everybody buying each other a present no matter how useless or inappropriate it turned out to be. Christmas morning had always entailed my sister and I going to our parent's bedroom where we would open our presents simultaneously, a ritual that was practised right up until the time when I failed to make it due to a hangover from the night before. Young children, albeit with the best of intentions are likely to make a parent squirm uncomfortably by getting a present that leaves them utterly bemused. I once bought my father a tobacco jar in the form of a skull that had clearly undergone a full lobotomy for the top which had an axe stuck in it (do not ask why) served as the lid. Okay, I admit it would not have been everybody's choice and probably set a new standard in bad taste, but I thought it was something special. The thing is I had managed to overlook the fact that he no longer smoked pipe tobacco. In those few moments of him un-wrapping my gift and making some affected appreciative grunts, it had already outlived its purpose. On another occasion when he was learning about basic geology on a Workers Education course my mother and I went in search of a book on geology to buy him as a Christmas present. The only one we could find was *The Principles of Physical Geology,* so we bought it for him as it had the word geology in the title. It turned out to be quite technical and quite advanced and remained the only book my father never read from cover to cover. We got the message after he went out and came back with a copy of the *Teach Yourself* series on geology. He had a few books in this series including *Teach Yourself Sex, Its*

Meaning and Purpose which considering he had already produced a son and daughter seemed to me to strongly suggest that he had already grasped both the meaning and the purpose. My mother said it was an embarrassment to have on the bookshelf and whatever would people think when they came into the room. The thing is unusual books were no strangers to my father's bookshelves, so setting aside his obvious books on travel, autobiographies, cannibalism and bizarre ceremonies and sexual practices of the orient there was also a collection of religious books including many by Lobsang Rampa. You may be forgiven for thinking that Lobsang Rampa is a type of tea and not the name of a writer who laboured under the impression that he was part man and part Tibetan lama. He sounds seriously mixed up to me, but then my mother often thought the same about my father when he proved to be one of the few people who would let a Mormon or a Jehovah's Witness past the threshold just so he could have a heated discussion with them.

His next literary port of call was Africa and books on Mungo Park, Livingstone and Hanning Speke to name but a few appeared on his bookshelves. The rest of the family took this as a clue in buying him, perhaps unwisely, his next lot of birthday and Christmas presents. Enter a model of an African slave girl complete with a grass skirt hiding her dignity, a genuine hand carved impala, a lethal looking hunting knife in a lion skin sheath that also doubled as a bull whip and a Zulu throwing spear, in fact almost everything he could have wished for from the world of utterly useless African artifacts that no grown man should be without. The way I see it is that a model of a slave girl is a poor compromise for the real thing, a carved wooden impala leaves me lost for words, a knife and bullwhip might have been of some use had my father been Indiana Jones which he most definitely was not, and he had missed the Zulu wars by quite a few years; so as presents go they were indeed quite pointless and served no purpose, ipso facto.

The spear which bore a sharp metal tip and a tuft of lion hair looked fairly authentic and more than capable of killing something or even someone. However, its credibility appeared decidedly shaky when I discovered it could be unscrewed in the middle to make two halves. I suppose it was made like this so visiting tourists could stow it in their hand baggage before flying home, otherwise stumbling down the aisle of an aircraft bearing a full length spear might prove to be a liability that could result in taking someone's eye out as the owner searched for his seat number in economy class. But the advantage of having a screw-apart spear at Rorke's Drift almost speaks for itself, for after you have thrown your weapon at the enemy, in this instance a gallant band of chorusing Welshmen, there is not much else you can do in filling in the time before getting shot. Whereas several screw-apart spears tucked into the waist band of your grass skirt means you could simply whip one out at will, assemble it quickly and get back into the fray, recharged and ready to kill. Now that surprise tactic would have been more than enough to wipe that smile off Michael Caine's face at the end of the film!

I think one of the most apparent differences between my boyhood and the times in which I now live is the lack of freedom for children. I would wander all day in woods, fields, quarries and railway sidings and only return home when I was hungry and my parents never had to worry about me. For today's youngsters it seems that behind every tree, bush or street corner lurks a paedophile, a knife wielding madman, or someone intent on stealing your mobile phone. The latter of course was never a problem during my childhood because nobody had a mobile phone. We did make our own out of two empty syrup tins and a length of string. How the world has changed.

When I was 15 I was allowed to go camping for the first time with a school friend. We decided to go near Baslow which coincidentally had just been in the news as the second body of a man had just been found close by and was dubbed the 'carbon-copy' murder. We gave little thought to being murdered in our tent so we went just the same. It rained for much of the time and we passed the time by lounging in the tent, talking and sucking on tubes of condensed milk. Now it could have been the condensed milk, or it could have been the tinned baked beans and sausages, the latter closely resembling two severed fingers in an advanced stage of putrefaction that became the cause of our unhealthy state. Either way we both developed stomach pains and returned home after three days with acute diarrhoea. Undaunted, some weeks later four of us set off along Chee Dale, waded through the freezing cold river (no namby-pamby stepping stones in our day) and set up our two tents in a field near Topley Pike. After a warming meal of partly burnt, partly uncooked and partly unrecognisable food I bedded down for the night. Because the tents lacked anything as advanced as a sewn-in groundsheet all sorts of creepy-crawly things with lots of legs came inside never having seen a tent before and no doubt wondering about the purpose of camping. My sleeping bag was merely a quilted down-filled tube with a drawstring at the top. In an effort to keep out the cold I pulled the bag over my head and drew the top together around my face. So far, so good. This worked fine until the following morning where a combination of overnight wriggling coupled with the physical properties of my bag meant the small aperture was now pressed hard against the top of my head and I was incarcerated inside. The sun had already warmed up the tent which in turn was heating up my sleeping bag and with little air inside I was slowly suffocating. I was in essence overheating and cooking in my own juices. For a few seconds I became aware that I was possibly sharing my bag with the Grim Reaper and became rather alarmed by my predicament as I lay there like a great green caterpillar in the throes of death. Trying to keep calm and gasping for air I managed to squirm down inside the bag sufficiently to pull the hole back over my face and breathe in some air. It took me ages to untie the knot and release myself, whereupon I crawled out of the tent dripping with sweat and took in the sweet smell of fresh air. I am sure it was this incident that has followed me through life making me fight off having anything over my face especially if I am on my back. This is why I had to apologise to the surgeon and the three nurses it took to hold me down after an operation some years ago when I came out of the anaesthetic, still only semi-conscious fighting and shouting all manner of abuse until they removed the mask from my face. My mates slept on totally unaware of my date with death. It would have been an unusual verdict for the coroner to proclaim my 'death by sleeping bag'.

Shortly after a farmer arrived and demanded two shillings, which we reluctantly handed over for camping in his field. We had camped by the main railway line to Derby and waved to a passing steam train as we lolled about in the morning sunshine. This period of relaxation was to be short lived as sparks from the engine had set fire to the embankment and with smoke and falling embers of burnt grass descending upon our tents the realisation that we had camped far too close to the line struck home. We leapt to our feet and began swiping wildly with T-shirts at the smouldering debris threatening to turn our tents into two piles of ash. And to think that only moments earlier we had paid two shillings for this! The following night we camped in Deepdale and well away from railways. We found a pickaxe in a cave and traded it with another farmer in exchange for a night's free camping. In the coming years we camped all over Derbyshire and further afield in Snowdonia, the Cairngorms and the Isle of Skye before life sent us on our different paths into the future. Today of course, there is no longer that kind of freedom to roam and pitch a tent almost at will whereever you fancied for the farmers and the law would soon be issuing you with a trespassing order. They were halcyon days.

By now I was 18 and had money in my pocket, so I could smoke cigarettes, drink pints of Watneys Red Barrel, have sex (still wishful thinking), shave, sport a DA (duck's arse) haircut and get myself into all manner of situations. So I went for it like a lamb to the slaughter and thereby hangs many a tale. I feel I should just relate this particular tale in defence of what might appear to be my questionable manhood. At 18 I did finally manage a first minor delve into the top of a girl's blouse. It was at a party in a large bell tent that had been pitched on top of Black Rocks near Cromford and liberally furnished with tins of Party Seven beer. I met this girl in the tent and after chatting for a time we decided to take a stroll in the woods and this is where it all went horribly wrong. We held hands as we strolled in the darkness of night, sensing the romance, sensing the passion and unexpectedly sensing the feeling of nothing beneath our feet as we both crashed headlong over an 8ft drop. Somehow this took the edge off things as we lay among the boulders and bracken, she complaining about her ripped tights and me nursing what felt like a broken thumb. We scrambled out of the undergrowth and sat on a rock. Trying to rekindle my lost moments of lust I clumsily foraged about inside her blouse and homed in on her left breast. At this point she gave a long sigh and said 'I don't know what my mother would say if she could see me now'. Now I may have been inexperienced in these matters but it struck me at the time that if a girl in the throes of being grappled can only think of her mother then that must be tantamount to saying that my technique was rubbish. I obviously needed to improve my modus operandi. I obviously needed to find some breasts to practice on, but that I am afraid will have to wait for another time.

Necessity moves us onwards and school days simply drift away into the rose-tinted past. We all change as indeed does the world around us. For my own part I rarely followed a 'nine to five' existence as I enjoyed for much of my time a life as a photographer, then a painter and illustrator. It allowed me considerable freedom and the excuse to travel. There was never a lack of subjects to photograph or later to paint and by the same token there was never a lack of places to visit in the world. Sadly, this rams home the inescapable fact that life can never be long enough in which to achieve everything, so I have to hope that longevity is on my side as to date I have been unable to come up with a formula for immortality. Not looking in a mirror partly helps.

Life for me has been a journey of exhilaration, stimulation, discovery, adventure and a roller coaster of emotions, but never total fulfilment. I always think there should be something else and the search for that elusive something else is endless and uncertain. Being able to package the memories of my schooldays has been an odyssey and a comfort insomuch as it will remain unchanged. It is stable, untouchable and cannot be altered. But what of all those lost, intense friendships formed in late adolescence during my years at the art school? We were, without doubt a select few who are scattered heaven knows where, for only once in my entire life have I met a person who attended the art school. In all my wanderings through all walks of life from Lords and Ladies, the rich and the famous to the humble roadside tramp and the homeless, nowhere have I come across a friend from the past except on one occasion.

About eight years after finishing school on a bleak wintery night I bumped into my good friend Pete on the blustery platform at Peterborough station. We were both waiting for different connecting trains and only had time to speak briefly before we caught trains to different destinations. For a short time a light was re-kindled on the past and somehow it was a small window looking out on the way our lives are led. That brief encounter was simply coincidence and not at all like the film of the same name as neither of us even in the poor visibility of the station lights looked remotely like Trevor Howard or Celia Johnson, and anyway the café was closed. It breached for a moment the invisible line drawn between the cossetted world of school and the raw reality of the world of work.

The only question that remains now is would I live my schooldays and childhood again if time allowed me the luxury of turning back the clock? I would answer most definitely yes, but I would have to make some serious changes such as eliminating a few teachers, one or two lessons, a number of bullies and not be so reticent about asking girls out for a date. In actual fact my reticence with girls did enable me to save to the point that in my mid-twenties I was able to buy and drive a brand new LandRover out from a showroom. Shortly afterwards I discovered that some girls seemed to show a penchant for bearded drivers of LandRovers, especially if they owned an Alsation dog. Well I had all three and it really did turn into a 'win-win' situation after all!